Second Edition

World Directory of Missionary Training Programmes

A Catalogue of Over 500 Missionary Training Programmes from around the world.

Raymond V. J. Windsor, Editor

Pasadena, California

© 1995
World Evangelical Fellowship
Missions Commission

All rights reserved. This book may not be reproduced or transmitted in any form or by any means, electronic or mechanical, including photocopying and recording, for any purpose, without the express written consent of the publisher.

William Carey Library is pleased to present this directory which has been prepared and provided by the editor as camera-ready copy.

Published by:
William Carey Library
P.O. Box 40129
Pasadena, CA 91114
USA
Telephone: (818) 798-0819

Cover Design: Jeff Northway

ISBN 0-87808-259-X
Printed in the United States of America

Contents

FOREWORD by William D. Taylor

Part 1 : ANALYSIS of DATA by Raymond V. J. Windsor

Part 2 : INDEX of 514 missionary training programs which are part of the IMTF Network. **

Part 3 : PROFILES of 281 of these programs.

** The IMTF Network

The International Missionary Training Fellowship (IMTF) was established in 1989 by the Missions Commission of the World Evangelical Fellowship.
It was conceived as "a global network of centres and individuals dedicated to training for cross-cultural ministries".

FOREWORD

by William D. Taylor
Director, WEF Missions Commission

Again we welcome a singular contribution to the global cause of Christ, the second edition of the World Directory of Mission Training Centres, published by the WEF Missions Commission in cooperation with William Carey Library.

Readers of the first edition will compare it to this new one, and should praise God for the significant growth of missionary training programs and centres worldwide during the last three years. We offer this volume with the prayer that it will be of particular assistance to all mission leaders in all mission-sending bases. We expect that as a result of this book much more strategic networking will take place, and God will lead some to significant inter-dependent partnerships in effective mission training.

A special word of appreciation goes to my veteran colleague and editor of this project, Dr. Raymond Windsor. It was his vision in 1988 that initially launched the Missions Commission into the significant projects and programs related to missionary training. His international perspective, first as a field missionary, then a mission agency director, followed by the years as Principal of All Nations Christian College, and subsequent travel world-wide, have all converged in his understanding of and commitment to effective equipping of the cross-cultural force.

Dr. Jonathan Lewis, another missionary colleague, serves as our publications coordinator. His vision, expertise and gifting have given our books greater relevance and visual attractiveness.

The Missions Commission serves the global Christian community within the broad parameters of WEF's vision statement:

MISSION STATEMENT
World Evangelical Fellowship and its member organizations exist to establish and help regional and national evangelical alliances enable and mobilize local churches and Christian organizations to disciple the nations for Christ.

The heart of the Missions Commission is articulated in the following two statements :

OUR PURPOSE : *To equip the Church and, in particular, the regional and national missions alliances to carry out the Great Commission.*

OUR VISION : *To serve as an international partnering-networking team that shares ideas, information and resources to empower the global missions movement to effectively train and send missionaries. We do this by affirming and facilitating the vision of regional and national missions leaders.*

The Commission is a global network of national missions leaders, many of whom have wider international roles. It dates to the early 70s and has had three directors:

Dr. Chun Chae Ok (1974-1979), a pioneer Korean woman missionary to Pakistan;

Dr. Theodore Williams (1979-1986) founder of the Indian Evangelical Mission & former Chairman of the Missions Commission; and

Dr. William D.Taylor (1986 to present), born in Costa Rica of missionary parents and a former career missionary to Guatemala.

From WEF's inception, a global passion has motivated its leadership.

The emergence of active, indigenous missionary movements in Asia, Africa, Latin America, the South Pacific, Caribbean and Middle East was the primary catalyst that led to the official launching of the Missions Commission in 1977.

Its fundamental intention was to address worldwide missions issues of common concern to its member bodies, with particular interest for these newly emerged and now maturing non-Western missionary movements.

It also serves as the primary global Evangelical missionary alliance, linking the continents in a spirit of inter-dependent partnership.

THE OBJECTIVES

1. To promote dynamic cooperation among existing and emerging national and regional missions associations, by providing a platform for :
    1.1 Expressing relational and informational networking
    1.2 Establishing national missions commissions
    1.3 Forging strategic alliances and partnerships

2. To strengthen and aid in the development of sending churches, training programs and support/shepherding structures by :

    2.1 Facilitating the use of experienced consultant resources
    2.2 Publishing and distributing vital information and didactic materials
    2.3 Facilitating the training of key Two Thirds World missions leaders

3. To address critical concerns of international Evangelical missions structures and their national and regional associations to achieve defined ends by :
    3.1 Convening strategic international conferences consultations
    3.2 Creating investigative task forces to address critical needs within global missions
    3.3 Administering projects and programs

If the WEF Missions Commission can be of service to you, please do not hesitate to write to us at any of the following addresses. May God bless you richly in your cross-cultural vision ministries.

WILLIAM D.TAYLOR

William D. Taylor, Director, WEF Missions Commission
4807 Palisade Drive, Austin, TX 78731, USA
TEL: 1 512 467 8431 FAX: 1 512 467 2841

International Headquarters, World Evangelical Fellowship
141 Middle Road, #05-05, GSM Building, Singapore 0718
TEL: 65 339 7900   FAX: 65 338 3756

North American Offices, World Evangelical Fellowship
P.O. Box WEF Wheaton, IL, 60189 USA
TEL: 708 668 0440   FAX: 708 669 0498

Part **ONE**

Analysis of data
by Dr. Raymond V. J. Windsor **

*** Raymond Windsor is Co-ordinator of the International Missionary Training Fellowship (IMTF) and a staff member of the Missions Commission of the World Evangelical Fellowship.*

ANALYSIS of DATA
by Dr. Raymond V. J. Windsor
Co-ordinator of the International Missionary Training Fellowship

A World Directory of Missionary Training Centres
was published in 1991 by the Missions Commission of the World Evangelical Fellowship, profiling 107 training centres. The centres were part of a global network established by the Missions Commission in 1989 to link *"centres and individuals dedicated to training for cross-cultural mission"*. The network is referred to as the International Missionary Training Fellowship (IMTF).

IMTF network

Centres actually training missionary candidates form the core group; but included also are Bible Colleges and Seminaries which offer courses on world missions or have degree programs in missiology.

The network has grown to include almost 1,000 individuals and just over 500 training programs. We have deliberately used the term 'program' rather than 'centre' in the title of this second edition, since many of the programs in the non-Western world are not as yet established centres. Many would justify the term 'emerging centre' but in using the term 'program' we are seeking to be widely inclusive of all who have made a beginning in training people for cross-cultural ministries.

Questionnaires were sent to the 514 programs in the network. 281 responses were received and the data provided by them is the basis for the Profiles included in this second edition directory.

Many of the responses are rather sketchy; but we have included their profile out of a desire to encourage them to develop along sound lines through networking actively with other centres from which they might learn.

Growth of non-Western programs

Of those which did not complete the questionnaire, many are emerging centres in the non-Western world, perhaps feeling inadequate to provide the sort of information requested.

Nevertheless the number of training programs in non-Western countries profiled in this directory represents an increase of around 100 programs since the first edition.

Of the non-Western programs profiled, only 30 existed pre -1975.

Over succeeding 5 year periods :

    1976-80 12 centres were established
    1981-85 23 centres were established
    1986-90 38 centres were established
    1991-   22 centres established thus far

One wonders how many more training programs exist outside the IMTF network. How much larger is the total, global training enterprise ? For example, only a minority of YWAM Schools of Frontier Missions are profiled here. Many mission agencies, especially denominational missions, have their own training programs. But the 514 programs listed in this directory must represent a substantial part of the whole.

Non-Western trainers

a) In non-Western programs :

While many non-Western centres still rely on Western trainers, there has been a steady growth in the number of non-Western trainers with some degree of field experience.

In many cases it would be more accurate to refer to "field exposure", since the experience is only that of leading field trips or visiting trainees on field assignment.

The following data emerge from the profiles regarding the number of non-Western teachers in different regions :

    96 of the 167 non-Western staff in African centres;
    100 of the 283 in Latin American centres;
    292 of the 440 in Asian centres ; and
    14 of the 29 in theWest Indies & South Pacific.

In round figures these total 1,000 non-Western trainers of whom half (500) have had field experience.

Highlighting the nations with the larger numbers -

    India   145 of 174 (83% with field experience)
    Nigeria   70 of 103 (68% with field experience)
    Korea   43 of 90 (48% with field experience)
    Brazil   34 of 106 (32% with field experience)
    Philippines 24 of 56 (43% with field experience)
    Singapore 24 of 29 (83% with field experience)
    Guatemala 23 of 59 (39% with field experience)

b) In Western programs

Few Western centres (only 32 of the 138 profiled) have appointed non-Westerners to their staff. Thus only 17 of the 63 American centres profiled and 6 of the 22 U.K. centres have non-Western teachers in their Missions Departments.

This may be due in part to a hesitation to take valuable resource personnel away from emerging centres in the Two Thirds World. However with the steadily growing pool of non-Western trainers with missionary experience, appointing some to teach in Western centres will likely become a highly significant development over the next decade.

Courses offered
The courses available are intentionally listed in only general categories. Clearly the next step, if more information is required, is to write direct to a particular centre for a Prospectus.

Learning styles

While the figures given in the questionnaires are only rough estimates, they allow of an interesting comparison between Western and non-Western centres in terms of the provision of non-formal learning experiences.

Formal education :	50% & less	60-70%	75-85%	90-100
North America	7	8	15	24
United Kingdom	5	6	6	1
India	2	7	1	5
Nigeria	4	5	2	1
Korea	3	3	1	5
Philippines	2	7	3	4
Brazil	5	12	2	1

North American centres clearly have the greatest emphasis on formal, class-room education - 45% of U S programs having 90-100% formal education. Contrast Nigeria with 8% of programs in this category and Brazil with 5% of programs.

We believe that there is a significant swing in Western countries towards a greater emphasis on non-formal learning experiences. We cannot document this from the above figures but the above data will serve as a base-line for future assessment.

Training ethos

Of the information in the profiles, the most interesting reading is the section on Training Ethos. Not all responses really address the ethos. However the submissions are printed virtually without editing. This is to keep faith with the invitation given to submit "what you would like other centres - and potential students - to know about your program and priorities."

A clear consensus emerging from these varied responses is that
1) there are three main areas in which missionaries need to be equipped : Spiritual formation, Ministry skills, and an understanding of Missiological principles.

2) non-formal and informal learning experiences are essential components of becoming "thoroughly equipped". II Timothy 3:17 NIV

Part **TWO**

Index
listing the 514 missionary training programs which are part of the IMTF Network.

Note : The programs are listed alphabetically by nation; and then, within each nation, alphabetically by title.

If a profile number is not provided the institution will not be found in the IMTF Network directory.

INSTITUTO BIBLICO BUENOS AIRES
La Pampa 2975, 1428 Capital Federal
Argentina Profile no. 1

INSTITUTO BIBLICO CORDOBA
Esquiv´ 247 B° General Paz, 5000 Cordoba
Argentina Profile no. 2

SCHOOL of FRONTIER MISSIONS (YWAM)
Casilla de Correo 595, 1000 Correo Central, Buenos Aires
Argentina Profile no. 3

SEMINARIO EVANGELICO INTERDENOMINACIONAL DE
TEOLOGIA Ave. Perón 1234, 1646 San Fernando, PCIA, Buenos Aires
Argentina Profile no. 4

SEMINARIO INT. BAUTISTA
Ramon Falcom 4080, 1407 Capital Federal
Argentina Profile no.

ASIA PACIFIC CHRISTIAN MISSION
PO Box 276 Preston, Vic 3072
Australia Profile no.

BIBLE COLLEGE of QUEENSLAND
1 Cross Street, Toowong, Brisbane Q 4066
Australia Profile no. 5

BIBLE COLLEGE of SOUTH AUSTRALIA
176 Wattle Street, Malvern, SA 5061
Australia Profile no. 6

BIBLE COLLEGE of VICTORIA, Centre for World Mission
PO Box 380 Lilydale, Vic. 3140
Australia Profile no. 7

EMMAUS BIBLE COLLEGE
PO Box 234 Epping, NSW 2121
Australia Profile no. 8

KINGSLEY COLLEGE
PO Box 125 Glenroy, Vic. 3046
Australia Profile no. 9

MORLING COLLEGE
120 Herring Road, Eastwood, NSW 2777
Australia Profile no. 10

PERTH BIBLE COLLEGE
Private Bag 3, Karrinyup, W.A. 6018
Australia Profile no. 11

SOUTH PACIFIC SUMMER INSTITUTE of LINGUISTICS
Graham Road, Kangaroo Ground, Vic. 3097
Australia Profile no. 12

St. ANDREW'S HALL,
190 The Avenue, Parkville, Vic 3052
Australia Profile no. 13

SYDNEY MISSIONARY & BIBLE COLLEGE
39 Badminton Road
Australia Profile no. 14

TAHLEE BIBLE COLLEGE
Karuah, NSW 2324
Australia Profile no. 15

WEC MISSIONARY TRAINING COLLEGE
PO Box 21, St. Leonards, Launceston, Tasmania 7250
Australia Profile no. 16

MISSIONARY TRAINING SCHOOL, Central European Teams (OM)
Postfach 61, A 1212 Vienna
Austria Profile no. 17

BANGLADESH THEOLOGICAL SEMINARY
7 Rashik Hazari Lane, GPO Box 78, Chittagong
Bangladesh Profile no.

BIBLE INSTITUTE
GPO Box 78 Chittagong 4000
Bangladesh Profile no.

BARBADOS BAPTIST COLLEGE
Fortescue, St Philip
Barbados Profile no.

BELGIAN CENTRE of BIBLICAL EDUCATION
1 Rue de la Chausee, 5990 Hamme-Mille
Belgium Profile no.

EVANGELICAL THEOLOGICAL FACULTY (Bijbelinstituut Belgie)
St. Jansbergsesteenweg 97, 3001 Heverlee-Leuven
Belgium Profile no. 18

INSTITUT BIBLIQUE BELGE
rue E. Vondervelde, 63, 6041 Gosselies
Belgium   Profile no. 19

OM BELGIUM
Nieuwevaart 288, 9000 Gent
Belgium   Profile no.

VOLLE EVANGELIE TRAININGS CENTRUM
Kapellelaan 332, 1860 Meise
Belgium   Profile no.

ECOLE DE MISSION INTERAFRICAINE AU BENIN (EMIAB)
B.P. 01 - 3285, Cotonou
Benin Republic   Profile no. 20

JUVENTUD CON UNA MISION (YWAM)
Casilla 4663 La Paz
Bolivia   Profile no.

ANTIOCH BIBLE SCHOOL, Missionary Training Course
CP 582 São Paulo - SP 01059 - 970
Brazil   Profile no. 21

ASSOCIACAO LINGUISTICA EVANGELICA MISSIONARIA (ALEM)
Brazil   Profile no.

AVANTE - Missao Evangelica Transcultural
CP 1261 Sao Paulo, SP CEP 01051-970
Brazil   Profile no.

BAPTIST CENTER for MISSIONARY TRAINING
Rua Senador Furtado 56, Praga da Bandeira, Rio de Janeiro 20270-020
Brazil   Profile no. 22

CENTRE FOR THE NATIONS
Caixa Postal 293 São Caetano do Sul, SP 09501-970
Brazil   Profile no. 23

CENTRO de TREINAMENTO MISSIONARIO BETANIA
Caixa Postal 174 Camaquã, RS 96180-000
Brazil   Profile no. 24

CENTRO de TREINAMENTO MISSIONARIO of the Church of God
Caixa Postal 14.139 São Paulo, SP 02731-000
Brazil   Profile no. 25

CENTRO DE TREINAMENTO MISSIONARIO (OM) Av. Andromeda
3621, Bosque dos Eucauptus, S.J. de Campos, SP 12233-000
Brazil   Profile no. 26

CENTRO EVANGÉLICO de MISSOES
Caixa Postal 53, Viçosa, MG   36570-000
Brazil   Profile no. 27

ESCOLA De MISSOES das ASSEMBLEIAS de DEUS - EMAD
Estrada Vicente de Carvalho 1083, Rio De Janeiro, RJ   21210-000
Brazil   Profile no.

INSTITUTO BIBLICO BETEL
C P 194 Joaoa Pessoa, PR, CEP 5800
Brazil   Profile no.

INSTITUTO BIBLICO EDUARDO
C P 12 Patrocinio, MG, CEP 38740
Brazil   Profile no.

INSTITUTO BIBLICO VIDA NOVA (CLAMIN)
Cxaixa Postal 166, Aquidauana MS, CEP 79200-000
Brazil   Profile no.

INSTITUTO TEOLOGIA QUADRANGULAR
Rua São Francisco - 204 - Centro, Curitiba, PR   80020-190
Brazil   Profile no. 28

KAIROS - ASS. PARA TREINAMENTO TRANSCULTURAL
Rua Angelo De Lucia, 228, Santo Amaro, São Paulo, SP   04756-000
Brazil   Profile no. 29

MISSAO AMEN   Rua Carlos Monte Verded, 25 - Boa Vista
Belo Horizonte MG   CEP 31060-350
Brazil   Profile no.

MISSAO MACEDONIA
C P 8411 Taguatinga, DF CEP 72021-9 70
Brazil   Profile no.

MTC LATINO AMERICANO
Caixa Postal 289 Montes Claros, MG 39400-970
Brazil   Profile no. 30

SAO PAULO BAPTIST THEOLOGICAL COLLEGE
Caixa Postal 70521 São Paulo, SP 05013- 990
Brazil   Profile no. 31

SCHOOL OF FRONTIER MISSIONS (YWAM)
Caixa Postal 524 Belo Horizonte, MG 30161-970
Brazil   Profile no. 32

SEMINARIO e INSTITUTO BIBLICO BETANIA
Caixa Postal 10 Altônia, PR 87550-000
Brazil   Profile no. 33

SEMINARIO EVANGELICO BETANIA
Av. Tancredo Neves 536, Cel. Fabriciano, MG 35170-074
Brazil   Profile no. 34

SEMINARIO JOVENS DA VERDADE
Caixa Postal 66 Aruja, SP 07400-970
Brazil   Profile no. 35

SEMINARIO TEOLOGICO BATISTA INDEPENDENTE
Curso de Missoes, Caixa Postal 1316 Campinas, SP 13001-970
Brazil   Profile no. 36

SEMINARIO TEOLOGICO DE GRAMADO
Caixa Postal 80 Gramado, RS 95670-000
Brazil   Profile no. 37

SEMINARIO TEOLOGICO EVANGELICO BETEL BRASILEIRO
Caixa Postal 8381 São Paulo, SP 01065-970
Brazil   Profile no. 38

SEMINARIO TEOLOGICO EVANGELICO PENIEL
Av. Maracana 63, Maracana, Rio De Janeiro, RJ 20271-110
Brazil   Profile no. 39

SEMINARIO TEOLOGICO MISSIONARIO DO NORTE
Caixa Postal 289 Montes Claros, M G 39400-970
Brazil   Profile no.

SENAMI
Estrada Vicente de Carvalho1083, Rio de Janeiro, RJ 21210
Brazil   Profile no.

WORD OF LIFE BIBLE SEMINARY
Caixa Postal 43 Atibaia, SP 12940 -000
Brazil   Profile no. 40

MISSIONARY CENTER
B.P. 6295 New-Bell, Douala
Cameroon   Profile no. 41

ACADIA DIVINITY COLLEGE
Wolfville, Nova Scotia B0P 1X0
Canada   Profile no. 42

ACTION INTERNATIONAL MINISTRIES
Canada Director, PO Box 1350 Three Hills, AB
Canada   Profile no.

BETHANY BIBLE COLLEGE, President
26 Western St., Sussex, NB E0E 1PO
Canada   Profile no.

BRIERCREST BIBLE COLLEGE, Intercultural Studies Department
510 College Drive, Caronport, SK S0H 0S0
Canada   Profile no. 43

CANADIAN BAPTIST SEMINARY
7600 Glover Road, Langley, BC V3A 6H4
Canada   Profile no. 44

CANADIAN CENTRE for WORLD MISSION
52 Canondale Crescent, Scarborough, ONT. M1W 2B1
Canada   Profile no.

CANADIAN THEOLOGICAL SEMINARY
4400 Fourth Ave., Regina, SK S4T 0H8
Canada   Profile no. 45

INTERNATIONAL TEAMS of CANADA
625 Wabanaki Drive, Unit 4, Kitchener, Ontario N2C 2G3
Canada   Profile no.

NORTHWEST BAPTIST COLLEGE
P O Box 790, Langley, BC V3A 8B8
Canada   Profile no. 46

ONTARIO BIBLE COLLEGE, Intercultural Studies
25 Ballyconnor Ct., North York, Ont M2M 4B3
Canada   Profile no. 47

ONTARIO THEOLOGICAL SEMINARY, Intercultural Focus
25 Ballyconnor Court, North York, ONT M2M 4B3
Canada   Profile no. 48

PRAIRIE BIBLE COLLEGE
Box 4000 Three Hills, AB T0M 2N0
Canada   Profile no. 49

PRAIRIE GRADUATE SCHOOL
CPO Box 30096 Calgary, AB T2H 2V8
Canada   Profile no. 50

PROVIDENCE COLLEGE & SEMINARY
May Institute of Mission Studies, Otterburne, Manitoba R0A 1G0
Canada   Profile no. 51

REGENT COLLEGE
5800 University Blvd, Vancouver, BC V6T 2E4
Canada   Profile no.

TRINITY WESTERN SEMINARY
7600 Glover Road, Langley, BC V3A 6H4
Canada   Profile no. 52

WORLD MISSIONARY TRAINING CENTER
c/o Clarence Knapp, 3384 Gladwin Road, Clearbrook, BC   V2S 7C9
Canada   Profile no. 53

BANGUI EVANGELICAL SCHOOL of THEOLOGY
BP 988 Bangui
Central African Republic   Profile no.

SHALOM EVANGELICAL SCHOOL OF THEOLOGY
BP 2006, N'Djamena
Chad   Profile no.

INSTITUTO TEOLOGICO AREA METROPOLTANA
Casilla 90 - Correo 22 Santiago
Chile   Profile no. 54

INSTITUTO TEOLOGICO DE TEMUCO
Casilla 11- D Temuco
Chile   Profile no. 55

JUVENTUD CON UNA MISION (YWAM)
Casilla 10161 Santiago 1
Chile   Profile no.

ASOCIACION NUEVAS TRIBUS
Carrera 74 #55-58 AA 16569, Santa Fe, Bogota
Colombia   Profile no.

CEMEN (KAIROS)
Apartado Postal 095152 Bogota, DC
Colombia   Profile no.

CENTRO DE ESTUDIOS BIBLICOS "BEREA"
Apartado Aéreo 48160 Santa Fe de Bogotá
Colombia   **Profile no. 56**

CRISALINCO Cra. 69 #53-89
AA 30898 Santa Fe, Bogota
Colombia   **Profile no.**

ETNAI Calle 75 #34-12
AA 54148 Santa Fe, Bogota
Colombia   **Profile no.**

INSTITUTO LINGUISTICO de VERANO, Technical Studies Dept.
A Aereo 100602, Bogota
Colombia   **Profile no.**

JUVENTUD CON UNA MISION (YWAM)
Calle 64 #5-61 AA 54595 Santa Fe, Bogota
Colombia   **Profile no.**

SEMINARIO BIBLICO DE COLOMBIA, Missiology Department
Apartado Aéreo 1141, Medellin
Colombia   **Profile no. 57**

COSTA RICA CENTER for WORLD MISSION
Aptdo 10250 - 1000 San Jose
Costa Rica   **Profile no.**

ESEPA SEMINARIO
Apartado 259-2350, San Francisco de Dos Rios, San Jose
Costa Rica   **Profile no.**

INSTITUTO MISIONOLOGICO de Las AMERICAS (IMDELA)
Aptdo 232, 1011Y Griega, San Jose
Costa Rica   **Profile no.**

BIBLIJSKO TEOLOSKI INSTITUT
P O Box 370, 54 103 Osijek
Croatia   **Profile no. 58**

LEVANT STUDY CENTRE
PO Box 2143, Paphos
Cyprus   **Profile no.**

DEPTO. DE EDUCACION TEOLOGICA
Casillo 8283 Quito
Ecuador   **Profile no.**

INST. SUPERIOR DE TEOLOGICA
Casilla 236A Quito
Ecuador   Profile no.

SEMINARIO BAUTISTA TEOLOGICO del ECUADOR
17-03-4724 Quito
Ecuador   Profile no. 59

SEMINARIO BIBLICO ALIANZA
Casilla 2006 Guayaquil
Ecuador   Profile no.

SEMINARIO BIBLICO ASAMBLEAS DE DIOS
10 de Agosto, cerca Marian de Jesus, Quito
Ecuador   Profile no.

SEMINARIO BIBLICO ASAMBLEAS DE DIOS
Casilla 5638 Guayaquil
Ecuador   Profile no.

MIES
Apdo. 05-12 Colonia Las Rosas 2, San Salvador
El Salvador   Profile no.

UNIVERSIDAD CRISTIANA DE LOS ASAMBLEOS DE DIOS
Facultad de Teologia/Misiones   Apdo. 2036 San Salvador
El Salvador   Profile no. 60

CHRISTIAN LEADERSHIP COLLEGE
PO Box 6915 Nasinu, Suva
Fiji Islands   Profile no. 61

GLOBAL MISSION BIBLE COLEGE
PO Box 596 Labasa, Vanua Levu
Fiji Islands   Profile no. 62

BETHANIE CENTRE de FORMATION MISSIONNAIRE
Le Chambon de Vorey, 43800 Vorey
France   Profile no. 63

BETHEL BIBLE INSTITUTE
B.P. 18,232 Libreville
Gabon   Profile no. 64

INSTITUT BIBLIQUE DE BETHEL
B.P. 13021 Libreville
Gabon, Central Africa   Profile no.

AGAPE EUROPE e.V.
Lettenbuck, 79424 Auggen-Hach
Germany   Profile no.

DEUTSCHE MISSIONS GEMEINSCHAFT
6920 Sinsheim, Buchenauerhof
Germany   Profile no.

FREIE HOCHSCHULE FÜR MISSION
Postfach 1129, D 70807 Korntal- Munchingen
Germany   Profile no. 65

M.V.DOULOS (Operation Mobilisation)
Postfach 1565, 74819 Mosbach
Germany   Profile no. 66

M.V. LOGOS II (Operation Mobilisation)
Postfach 1565, 74819 Mosbach
Germany   Profile no. 67

MISSIONSHAUS BIBELSCHULE WIEDENEST
Postfach 1360, Olperstrasse 10, 51702 Bergneustadt
Germany   Profile no. 68

THEOLOGISCHES SEMINAR der LIEBENZELLER MISSION
PO Box 1240, 75375 Bad Liebenzell
Germany   Profile no. 69

CHRISTIAN SERVICE COLLEGE
PO Box 3110 Kumasi
Ghana   Profile no. 70

GHANA CHRISTIAN COLLEGE
PO Box 5722 Accra
Ghana   Profile no. 71

GHANA EVANGELICAL MISSIONS INSTITUTE
P O Box 2632 Accra
Ghana   Profile no.

GILLBT
PO Box 7271 Accra North
Ghana   Profile no.

WORLD LINK UNIVERSITY
Box 2632 Accra
Ghana   Profile no. 72

CENTRAL AMERICAN CENTER FOR MISSIONARY EDUCATION
(CEMCA)   Apdo. 129 Cod. 01901, Guatemala City
Guatemala   Profile no. 73

CENTRO DE CAPACITACION MISIONERA
Av. Centro America 21-31, zona 1, Guatemala City
Guatemala   Profile no.

CENTRO DE ENTRANAMIENTO DE MISIONES
INTERNACIONALES
Guatemala   Profile no.

CENTRO DE EVANGELIZACION Y CAPACITACION MISIOLOGICA
(CECAM)   6a. Avenida "A" 4-60 zona 1. Guatemala ciudad. 01001
Guatemala   Profile no. 74

CURSO DE MISIONES POR CORRESPONDENCIA
Apartado Postal 555 - A, Guatemala City
Guatemala   Profile no. 75

ESCUELA DE MISIONES, Asambleas de Dios
28 calle, Ave. Elena 0-52 zona 3, Guatemala
Guatemala   Profile no.

FACULTAD TEOLOGICA PENTECOSTAL
Apdo. Postal 307, Guatemala City 01901
Guatemala   Profile no. 76

INSTITUTO LINGUISTICO de VERANO (ILV)
7a Ave. 32 - 31, zona 11 Guatemala
Guatemala   Profile no.

JUVENTUD CON UNA MISION (YWAM)
Apdo. Postal 77 "I" Guatemala 01907
Guatemala   Profile no.

PERSPECTIVAS CONEMM
Apartado 28, 01901 Guatemala City
Guatemala   Profile no. 77

PROYECTO MIES
Calle Mariscal 12 - 15, zona 11, Guatemala
Guatemala   Profile no.

SEMINARIO TEOLOGICO CENTRO AMERICANO
Apdo. 213, 01901 Guatemala City
Guatemala   Profile no. 78

CARIBBEAN MISSIONARY TRAINING CENTER
#23 Rue Boudierre, Port-au-Prince
Haiti Profile no.

ALLIANCE BIBLE SEMINARY
22 Peak Road, Cheung Chau
Hong Kong Profile no. 79

CHINA GRADUATE SCHOOL of THEOLOGY
5 Devon Road, Kowloon
Hong Kong Profile no.

CHINA MISSION TRAINING INSTITUTE, Chinese Mission
Seminary
Hong Kong Profile no. 80

HONG KONG BIBLE SEMINARY
17 Cumberland Road, Kowloon Tong
Hong Kong Profile no.

OM LOVE ASIA
GPO Box 12507
Hong Kong Profile no.

ADVANCED LEADERSHIP TRAINING CENTRE, 24/A Bhagwan
Sahai Complex, Opp. DDA (SFS) Anupam Apts., Neb Sarai Rd.,New
India Profile no.

AL BASHIR
P O Bag 13 Patel Nagar, New Delhi   110 008
India Profile no.

BEERSHEBA GOSPEL TRAINING CENTRE
Waterworks Road, Pathankot   145 001
India Profile no. 81

BETHEL BIBLE INSTITUTE
Danishpet, Salem District, Tamil Nadu   636 364
India Profile no.

CHRIST'S DISCIPLES TRAINING INSTITUTE
Kadihati P O Ganti (N) via Ganganagar, 24 Parganas, W. Bengal 743
India Profile no. 82

CHURCH GROWTH RESEARCH CENTRE, McGavran Institute
Post Bag 512 Egmore, Madras   600 008
India Profile no. 83

CHURCH ON THE ROCK THEOLOGICAL SEMINARY
Dora Thota, Bhimili P.O. Box 3, Dist. Vizag, A.P. 531 163
India **Profile no. 84**

EASTERN THEOLOGICAL COLLEGE
P O Rajabari, Jorhat, Assam 785 014
India **Profile no.**

Faith Institute of Evangelism (FIRE)
Prakashnagar, Narasaraopet, Guntur District A.P. 522 602
India **Profile no.**

FAITH THEOLOGICAL SEMINARY
P O Box No. 1 Manakala, Dist. Pathanamthitta, Adoor, Kerala 691 551
India **Profile no. 85**

FELLOWSHIP FOR NEIGHBOURS INDIA (FFNI)
PO Box 611, Vellore, TN 632 006
India **Profile no.**

FILADELFIA BIBLE COLLEGE
Rani Road, opp. Sanjay Park, Udaipur, Rajasthan 313 001
India **Profile no. 86**

Friends Missionary Prayer Band
110 Baracca Road, Kilpauk, Madras 600 010
India **Profile no.**

FRONTIER MISSIONS CENTRE (YWAM)
G P O Box 127 Pune, Maharashtra 411 001
India **Profile no. 87**

HOWRAH TRAINING CENTRE JKPS Flat #C-4 Fourth Floor
33/31 Nafar Chandra Das Road, Calcutta 700 034
India **Profile no.**

INDIA CENTRE FOR EVERY PEOPLE (O.M. INDIA) Logos Bhavan,
Medchal Road, Jeedimetla, Secunderabad, A.P. 500 855
India **Profile no. 88**

INDIAN INSTITUTE for CROSS- CULTURAL COMMUNICATION,
Post Box 376, Andra University P.O., Visakhapatanam, AP 530 003
India **Profile no. 89**

INDIAN INSTITUTE of MULTI-CULTURAL STUDIES
204 P L Banerjee Road, Lalgarh, Madhupur, Dist. Deoghar, Bihar 815
India **Profile no. 90**

JUBILEE MEMORIAL BIBLE COLLEGE
Post Box 3465 Anna Nagar West, Madras   600 040
India   **Profile no. 91**

LUTHER NEW THEOLOGICAL COLLEGE
Kulhan P O Challang, Sahastradhara Road, Dehra Dun, UP 248 001
India   **Profile no. 92**

MISSIONARY TRAINING INSTITUTE, Navajeevodayam Centre
PO Box 16, Tiruvalla, Kerala   689 101
India   **Profile no. 93**

NAGALAND MISSIONARY MOVEMENT
P O Box 39 Dimapur, Nagaland
India   **Profile no.**

NEW INDIA EVANGELISTIC ASSOCIATION
H-5 Jawahar Nagar, Trivandrum, Kerala   695 041
India   **Profile no.**

ORISSA SCHOOL OF EVANGELISM
P O Bag No. 10, B.C. Sen Road, Balasore, Orissa 756 001
India   **Profile no. 94**

OUTREACH LEADERSHIP TRAINING CENTRE
P O Box 44 Dimapur, Nagaland   797 112
India   **Profile no. 95**

OUTREACH TRAINING INSTITUTE
IEM, 7 Langford Road, Bangalore 560 025
India   **Profile no. 96**

RAJASTHAN BIBLE INSTITUTE
Mubarak Bagh, Jaipur, Rajasthan   302 006
India   **Profile no.**

Secretary, Synod Mission Board, Mizo Presbyterian Church
Aizawl, Mizoram   796 001
India   **Profile no.**

SOUL WINNERS BIBLE SEMINARY (SISWA)
Post Box 3463, Anna Nagar, Madras   600 040
India   **Profile no. 97**

SOUTH ASIA INSTITUTE OF ADVANCED CHRISTIAN STUDIES
(SAIACS) Box 7747 Kothanur P.O. , Bangalore
India   **Profile no. 98**

SOUTH INDIA BIBLE SEMINARY
Bangarapet, Karnataka 563 114
India   Profile no.

SPICER MEMORIAL COLLEGE of Seventh Day Adventists
Aundh Road, Ganashkhind, Pune 411 007
India   Profile no.

TRIVANDRUM BIBLE COLLEGE   (New Life Ministries)
P O Box 3505 Sreekariyam, Trivandrum, Kerala   695 017
India   Profile no.

UNION BIBLICAL SEMINARY, Centre for Mission Studies
Post Box 1425 Bibvewadi, Pune   411 037
India   Profile no. 99

YAVATMAL COLLEGE for LEADERSHIP TRAINING,
Post Box 25, Yavatmal, Maharashtra 445 001
India   Profile no. 100

EVANGELICAL THEOLOGICAL SEMINARY of INDONESIA
JL. Sala Km. 11, Kotak Pos. No.4 / YKAP, Yogyakarta
Indonesia   Profile no. 101

GLOBE MISSIONARY EVANGELISM
Kotak Pos 1220, Medan, Sumut 20 001
Indonesia   Profile no.

INSTITUT ALKITAB "RHEMA"
Jl Hasanuddin No.6, Medan, Sumut
Indonesia   Profile no. 102

PUSET LATIHAN PENGINJILAN
PO Box 239 Sentani, Irian Jaya
Indonesia   Profile no.

ECOLE MISSIONNAIRE du PLEIN EVANGILE en COTE d'IVOIRE
21 B.P. 108, Abidjan 21
Ivory Coast, West Africa   Profile no. 103

L'INSTITUT IINTERAFRICAIN de FORMATION MISSIONAIRE
(L.I.F.M.) 08 B.P. 1810 Abidjan 08
Ivory Coast, West Africa   Profile no.

CARIBBEAN GRADUATE SCHOOL of THEOLOGY
PO Box 121 Constant Spring, Kingston 8
Jamaica   Profile no. 104

JAMAICAN THEOLOGICAL SEMINARY
114 West Avenue, Kingston 8
Jamaica Profile no.

IMMANUEL BIBLE TRAINING COLLEGE
1194-1 Nishihassaku-cho, Midori-ku, Yokohama 227
Japan Profile no. 105

JAPAN SUMMER INSTITUTE OF LINGUISTICS
4-31-7 Hamadayama, Suginami-ku, Tokyo 168
Japan Profile no. 106

MISSIONARY TRAINING CENTER
P O Box 1 Takaku Ots, Nasu-machi, Tochigi-ken
Japan Profile no. 107

AFRICA INLAND CHURCH MISSIONARY COLLEGE
P O Box 3718, Eldoret
Kenya Profile no. 108

INTERNATIONAL CHRISTIAN MINISTRIES
PO Box 1284 Kitale
Kenya Profile no.

NAIROBI EVANGELICAL GRADUATE SCHOOL of THEOLOGY
PO Box 24 686 Karen, Nairobi
Kenya Profile no. 109

NAIROBI INTERNATIONAL SCHOOL OF THEOLOGY
P O Box 60954, Nairobi
Kenya Profile no. 110

SCHOOL OF MISSIONS, Eastern Region
Association of Evangelicals of Africa (AEA) P O Box 49332 Nairobi
Kenya Profile no. 111

ASIA GRADUATE SCHOOL of THEOLOGY
187 Choong-ro, 3Ka , Sudaemoon-ku , Seoul 120-013
Korea Profile no.

ASIAN CENTER for THEOLOGICAL STUDIES & MISSION - ACTS
187 Choongjeong-Ro 3ga, Sudaemoon-Gu, Seoul 120-751
Korea Profile no. 112

CROSS-CULTURAL MISSIONARY TRAINING INSTITUTE
395-153 Suhkyo-dong, Mapo-ku, Seoul 121-210
Korea Profile no. 113

EAST WEST CENTER for MISSIONS, RESEARCH and
DEVELOPMENT, 110-1 Wolmoon, Paltan, Hwasung, Kunggi-do
Korea   **Profile no. 114**

FULL GOSPEL WORLD MISSIONARY TRAINING CENTER
Yoido Full Gospel Church, P O Box 7 Seoul
Korea   **Profile no. 115**

GLOBAL MISSIONARY TRAINING CENTER
231-188 Mok 2 Dong, Yang Chun Ku, Seoul 158-052
Korea   **Profile no. 116**

GLOBAL PROFESSIONALS TRAINING INSTITUTE
Kang Nam P O Box 1052 Seoul 135-610
Korea   **Profile no. 117**

HAPDONG SEMINARY
New Banpo, Apt.16-207, Sucho-ku, Seoul
Korea   **Profile no.**

INSTITUTE of ISLAMIC STUDIES
CPO Box 9024, Seoul 100 - 690
Korea   **Profile no. 118**

INTERNATIONAL MISSIONARY TRAINING INSTITUTE
PO Box 93, Sudaimoon, Seoul   120-600
Korea   **Profile no. 119**

KEHC MISSION HOME
890-56 Daechi-dong, Kangnam-ku, Seoul 138-160
Korea   **Profile no. 120**

KOREA BAPTIST THEOLOGICAL SEMINARY
San 14, Hakidong Yusung, Taejon 305-358
Korea   **Profile no.**

KOREA CAMPUS CRUSADE for CHRIST
15-5 Jung-dong, Choong-ku, Seoul 100-120
Korea   **Profile no.**

KOREA MISSIONARY TRAINING INSTITUTE
277-7 Choeup-dong, Jin-ku, Pusan 614-080
Korea   **Profile no.**

KOREAN CENTER for WORLD MISSIONS
55 Yang Jai-dong, Sucho-ku, Seoul 137-130
Korea   **Profile no. 121**

KOREAN WORLD MISSIONS TRAINING INSTITUTE
P O Box 94 Choong Jongno, Seoul 120-650
Korea   Profile no. 122

KOSIN MISSIONARY TRAINING INSTITUTE (KMTI)
243 - 17 Jungli-Dong, Daedug-Gu, Daejeon City 306-050
Korea   Profile no. 123

MISSIONARY TRAINING INSTITUTE, Presbyterian Church of Korea
58 - 10 Banpo-dong, Seocho-ku, Seoul 137-040
Korea   Profile no. 124

OM MISSIONARY TRAINING CENTRE
PO Box 120 Kang Nam , Seoul
Korea   Profile no. 125

PRESBYTERIAN CHURCH in KOREA, General Assembly
1007-3 Daichi 3-dong, Kangnam-ku, Seoul 135 - 283
Korea   Profile no.

PRESBYTERIAN THEOLOGICAL SEMINARY, Center for World
Mission, 353 Kwang jang-dong, Sungdong-ku, Seoul 133-210
Korea   Profile no.

SEOUL THEOLOGICAL COLLEGE & SEMINARY
101 Sosa-dong, Boochun, Kyunggi-do   422-050
Korea   Profile no.

The CHONG SHIN COLLEGE & THEOLOGICAL SEMINARY,
 San 31-3. SadangDong, DongJak-Ku, Seoul 156-763
Korea   Profile no.

WORLD MISSION TRAINING CENTER, Korea Baptist Theological
Seminary, San 14, Haki-Dong, Yusung, Taejon 305-358
Korea   Profile no. 126

WORLD MISSIONARY TRAINING INSTITUTE
304-43 Sajik-dong, Jongro-ku, Seoul 110-054
Korea   Profile no.

YWAM Nam Seoul,
PO Box 131 Seoul 151-600
Korea   Profile no.

CALVARY CHARISMATIC CENTRE
P O Box 14235, 88848 Kota Kinabalu, Sabah
Malaysia   Profile no.

IEM, Apartado M- 8580
DF 06000
Mexico   **Profile no.**

INSTITUTO BETANIA, A.C.
Apdo. Postal 27, C.P. 78700 Matehuala, S.L.P.
Mexico   **Profile no. 127**

SEMINARIO BAUTISTA
Apdo. 266 Adrn.2, cd. Satelite
Mexico   **Profile no.**

SEMINARIO BIBLICO MEXICANO
Apdo. Post. 766, Hermosillo, Sonora
Mexico   **Profile no.**

WORLD MISSIONS INSTITUTE of MEXICO
Apartado 798, Morelia, Michoacan 58000
Mexico   **Profile no. 128**

SEMINARIO TEOLOGICO EVANGELICO de MOZAMBIQUE
CP 2433 Maputo
Mozambique   **Profile no.**

KAYIN BAPTIST THEOLOGICAL INSTITUTE
Seminary Hill, Insein, Yangon
Myanmar   **Profile no.**

CENTRALE PINKSTER BIJBELSCHOOL
Barneveldse weg 11, 6741 LH Lunteren
Netherlands   **Profile no. 129**

EVANGELISCHE BIJBEL SCHOOL
Postbus 171, 3940 AD Doorn
Netherlands   **Profile no. 130**

IN DE RUIMTE BIJBELSCHOOL
Postbus 16, 3760 AA Soest
Netherlands   **Profile no. 131**

REFORMATORISCHE BIJBELSCHOOL
Krakelingen weg 10, 3707 HV Zeist
Netherlands   **Profile no.**

SCHOOL of FRONTIER MISSIONS "Heidebeek" (YWAM)
Mussen kampse weg 32, 8181 PK Heerde
Netherlands   **Profile no. 132**

The EURO MISSIONARY TRAINING COLLEGE
Hagelkruisstraat 19, 5835 BD Beugen
Netherlands Profile no. 133

Trainingschool voor Dienst in het Midden oosten (Near East Ministry) Postbus 30, 3780 BA Voorthuizen
Netherlands Profile no.

TYNDALE THEOLOGICAL SEMINARY
Egelantier straat 1, 1171 JM Badhoevedorp
Netherlands Profile no. 134

VORMING en AKTIE
Arnhemseweg 57, 6711 GS Ede
Netherlands Profile no.

VORMINGSCENTRUM JANG en VRIJ
Vleerdamsedijk 15, 3235 NV Rockanje
Netherlands Profile no.

BIBLE COLLEGE of NEW ZEALAND, Department of Mission Studies
Private Bag, Henderson, Auckland 8
New Zealand Profile no. 135

CENTRE for MISSION DIRECTION
P O Box 31-146, Ilam, Christchurch 8030
New Zealand Profile no. 136

FAITH BIBLE COLLEGE
Private Bag, Tauranga
New Zealand Profile no. 137

GLO BIBLE & MISSIONARY COLLEGE
P O Box 390, Te Awamutu
New Zealand Profile no. 138

NEW COVENANT INTERNATIONAL BIBLE COLLEGE
P O Box 13-470, Onehunga, Auckland 6
New Zealand Profile no. 139

NEW ZEALAND ASSEMBLY BIBLE SCHOOL
20 Palmer Avenue, Kelston, Auckland
New Zealand Profile no. 140

AGAPE SCHOOL of MISSIONS
P O Box 80 Barkin Ladi, Plateau State
Nigeria Profile no. 141

ASSEMBLIES of GOD DIVINITY SCHOOL of NIGERIA
P O Box 50 Old Umahia, Abia State
Nigeria **Profile no.**

BIBLE & MISSIONARY THEOLOGICAL COLLEGE
PO Box 26 Ikot Abasi, Akwa, Ibom State
Nigeria **Profile no.**

CALVARY INTERNATIONAL BIBLE COLLEGE
PO Box 4390, Ibadan, Oyo State
Nigeria **Profile no.**

CALVARY MINISTRIES, SCHOOL of MISSIONS,
PO Box 6001, Jos, Plateau State
Nigeria **Profile no. 142**

CHRISTAC SCHOOL of MISSIONS & DEVELOPMENT
P O Box 1293 Sagamu, Ogun State
Nigeria **Profile no. 143**

CHRISTIAN LEADERSHIP & MISSIONARY TRAINING INSTITUTE
GPO Box 10335, Ibadan, Oyo State
Nigeria **Profile no. 144**

CHRISTIAN LEADERSHIP & MISSIONS INSTITUTE
PO Box 2449 Warri
Nigeria **Profile no. 145**

CHRISTIAN MISSIONARY FOUNDATION, School of Missions
U. I. P O Box 9890 Ibadan
Nigeria **Profile no. 146**

ECWA THEOLOGICAL SEMINARY
P O Box 20 Igbaja, via Ilorin, Kwara State
Nigeria **Profile no.**

EVANGEL BIBLE COLLEGE
129 Okota Road, Okoto, Isolo, Lagos
Nigeria **Profile no.**

EVANGELICAL MISSIONARY SOCIETY of ECWA
PO Box 63, Jos, Plateau State
Nigeria **Profile no.**

GOFAMINT - Gospel Faith Mission Int., Missions Department
U..I. P O Box 20956 Ibadan, Oyo State
Nigeria **Profile no. 147**

GOSPEL BIBLE COLLEGE
Box 270 Okitipupa, Ondo State
Nigeria   **Profile no.**

LIFE TRAINING CENTRE
P O Box 3, Dekina, Kogi State
Nigeria   **Profile no.**

LIFE TRAINING CENTRE
PO Box 3 Dekina, Kogi State
Nigeria   **Profile no. 148**

LIVING STONES MINISTRIES
P O Box 2905 Mushin, Lagos
Nigeria   **Profile no.**

NIGERIA CENTRE FOR WORLD MISSION
G P O Box 221, Dugbe, Ibadan, Oyo State
Nigeria   **Profile no. 149**

NIGERIA EVANGELICAL MISSIONARY INSTITUTE (NEMI)
PO Box 5878, Jos, Plateau State
Nigeria   **Profile no. 150**

SAMUEL BILL THEOLOGICAL COLLEGE
PO Box 34 Abak, Akwa, Ibom State
Nigeria   **Profile no.**

SCHOOL of DISCIPLESHIP and MISSIONS (SCODAM)
GPO Box1550 Ibadan, Oyo State
Nigeria   **Profile no. 151**

SCHOOL OF MISSIONARY STUDIES
UIPO Box 19488 Ibadan, Oyo State
Nigeria   **Profile no. 152**

SOULS HARVESTERS MINISTRIES INC.
PO Box 2449 Warri, Delta State
Nigeria   **Profile no.**

THE REDEEMED CHRISTIAN BIBLE SCHOOL
P O Box 172 Ebute-Metta, Lagos
Nigeria   **Profile no.**

THE REDEEMED CHRISTIAN SCHOOL of MISSIONS
P O Box 220 Ede, Osun State
Nigeria   **Profile no. 153**

TRAINING IN DISCIPLESHIP and MISSIONS
P O Box 80 Barkin Ladi, Plateau State
Nigeria Profile no.

UNITED MISSIONARY THEOLOGICAL COLLEGE
P O Box 171 Ilorin, Kwara State
Nigeria Profile no. 154

WORD OF LIFE TRAINING CENTRE
63 oyemekun Road, Akure, Ondo State
Nigeria Profile no.

WORLD OUTREACH BIBLE INSTITUTE
P O Box 462 Sulejah, Niger State
Nigeria Profile no. 155

FJELLHAUG MISSION SEMINARY
Sinsenveien 15, N- 0572 Oslo
Norway Profile no. 156

GÅ UT SENTERET, Norwegian Santal Mission
2090 Hurdal
Norway Profile no. 157

The SCHOOL of MISSION & THEOLOGY
Misjonsveien 34, 4024 Stavanger
Norway Profile no. 158

BETHEL BIBLE COLLEGE
P O Box 6166 Boroko
Papua New Guinea Profile no. 159

CHRISTIAN LEADERS' TRAINING COLLEGE
PO Box 382 Mt Hagen, WHP
Papua New Guinea Profile no. 160

CHRISTIAN TRAINING CENTRE
Free Mail Bag Service, Boroko
Papua New Guinea Profile no. 161

PAPUA NEW GUINEA MISSIONARY ASSOCIATION
PO Box 6609 Boroko, Port Moresby
Papua New Guinea Profile no.

CENTRO de EVANGELISMO y MISIONES BETANIA
Casilla de Correo 3045 Asunción
Paraguay Profile no. 162

JUVENTIA CON UNA MISION (YWAM)
Casilla de Correo 1961, Asuncion
Paraguay   Profile no.

CENTRO DE CAPACITACION MISIONERA (PETRA)
Apdo. 3828 Lima 100
Peru   Profile no.

CENTRO EVANGELICO de MISIOLOGIA
Casilla 2492 Lima 100
Peru   Profile no.

ESCUELA MISIOLOGICA LATINO AMERICANA
Apartado 1488 Lima 100
Peru   Profile no. 163

INSTITUTO BIBLICO ALIANZA
Prol.Cayetano Heredia 151, Pueblo Libre, Lima 21
Peru   Profile no.

INSTITUTO MISIOLOGICO AMAZONICO
Apartado 1710 Lima 100
Peru   Profile no. 164

INTITUTO BIBLICO DE LIMA
Jr. Nazca 148, Jesus Maria , Lima 11
Peru   Profile no.

INTITUTO PENTECOSTAL del PERU
Apdo. 4561 Lima 100
Peru   Profile no.

JUVENTUD CON UNA MISION (YWAM)
Apartado 1710 Lima 100
Peru   Profile no.

SEGADORES
Apdo. 1710, Jr.Moquegua 628, Of. 401, Lima 100
Peru   Profile no.

SEMINARIO BIBLICO ANDINO
Av. Colombia 325, Pueblo Libre, Lima 21
Peru   Profile no.

SEMINARIO EVANGELICO de LIMA
Escuela Superior de Teologia, Apdo 207 Lima 12
Peru   Profile no.

ALLIANCE BIBLICAL SEMINARY
CPO Box 1095, 1099 Manila
Philippines Profile no. 165

ASIA PACIFIC THEOLOGICAL SEMINARY (AOG)
P O Box 377 Baguio City, 2600
Philippines Profile no. 166

ASIAN SEMINARY OF CHRISTIAN MINISTRIES
P O Box 133 MCPO, Makati, 1299 Metro Manila
Philippines Profile no. 167

ASIAN THEOLOGICAL SEMINARY, Cross-cultural Studies program
Q. C. C P O Box 1454, Quezon City 1154
Philippines Profile no. 168

BAPTIST BIBLE SEMINARY & INSTITUTE
P O Box 2800 Manila 1099
Philippines Profile no.

CENTRAL PHILIPPINE UNIVERSITY, College of Theology
Jaro Iloilo 5000
Philippines Profile no.

CHARISMATIC OUTREACH MINISTRIES FOUNDATION INC.
P O Box 596 Greenhills, Metro Manila 3113
Philippines Profile no.

CONSERVATIVE BAPTIST BIBLE COLLEGE
P O Box 1594 Manila 1099
Philippines Profile no.

DISCIPLESHIP TRAINING SCHOOL (YWAM)
P O Box 1195 Ortigas Center, 1651 Pasig, Metro Manila
Philippines Profile no. 169

FEBIAS COLLEGE of BIBLE
P O Box 2, 1405 Valenzuela, Metro Manila
Philippines Profile no.

GLOBAL CHALLENGE
Mayflower Plaza PO Box 260, Mandaluyong, Metro Manila 1501
Philippines Profile no.

GREAT COMMISSION MISSIONARY TRAINING CENTER
PO Box 12838, Ortigas Center Post Office, 1605 Pasig, Metro Manila
Philippines Profile no. 170

INTERNATIONAL SCHOOL OF THEOLOGY - ASIA
ACPO Box 51, Quezon City 1109
Philippines   **Profile no.**

INTERNATIONAL TRAINING INSTITUTE for MISSIONS
ACPO Box 128 Quezon City
Philippines   **Profile no. 171**

LOMMASSON ALLIANCE BIBLE INSTITUTE
Lapuyan, Zamboanga del Sur 7037
Philippines   **Profile no. 172**

NEW TRIBES SCHOOL OF MISSIONS
P O Box 2570 Manila
Philippines   **Profile no.**

PHILIPPINE BAPTIST THEOLOGICAL SEMINARY
P O Box 7 Baguio City 2600
Philippines   **Profile no.**

PHILIPPINE BIBLE COLEGE
P O Box 114 Baguio City
Philippines   **Profile no.**

PHILIPPINE MISSIONARY INSTITUTE
Biga, Silang, Cavite 2702
Philippines   **Profile no. 173**

Philippine Resources of Christian Literature & Information Ministries
(PROCLAIM) - 15 Gueguesangen, Sta. Barbara, Pangasinan 2419
Philippines   **Profile no. 174**

THE WORLD MISSION INSTITUTE
Blooming Hills subd., Kaytikling Taytay, 1901 Rizal
Philippines   **Profile no.**

VISAYAN NAZARENE BIBLE COLLEGE
P O Box 261 Cebu City 6000
Philippines   **Profile no.**

WESLEYAN BIBLE COLLEGE
Rosales, Pangasinan 0739
Philippines   **Profile no.**

YOUTH WITH A MISSION
P O Box 1195 Ortigas Center, 1651 Pasig, M.M.
Philippines   **Profile no.**

SIERRA LEONE BIBLE COLLEGE
PO Box 890 Freetown
Sierra Leone, West Africa   Profile no.

ASIA EVANGELISTIC FELLOWSHIP, School of Missions &
Evangelism
Singapore   Profile no. 175

ASIAN CROSS CULTURAL TRAINING INSTITUTE
Raffles City P O Box 1052 Singapore 9117
Singapore   Profile no. 176

BAPTIST THEOLOGICAL SEMINARY
1 Cambridge Road, Singapore 0821
Singapore   Profile no.

BETHANY SCHOOL of MISSIONS
Raffles City PO Box 143 Singapore 9117
Singapore   Profile no. 177

DISCIPLESHIP TRAINING CENTRE
33A Chancery Lane, Singapore 1130
Singapore   Profile no. 178

HWE HAI GOSPEL BIBLE INSTITUTE
c/o CNEC in SE Asia, PO Box 771, Toa Payoh North, Singapore 9131
Singapore   Profile no.

O C MINISTRIES Asia
Bras Basah PO Box 0311, Singapore 9118
Singapore   Profile no.

SINGAPORE BIBLE COLLEGE, Diploma in Intercultural Ministry
Farrer Road PO Box 257 Singapore 9128
Singapore   Profile no. 179

The NAVIGATORS Singapore
Marine Parade PO Box 643 Singapore
Singapore   Profile no.

THEOLOGICAL CENTRE for ASIA
Farrer Road PO Box 90 Singapore 9128
Singapore   Profile no. 180

AFRICA SCHOOL OF MISSIONS
P O Box 439 White River, 1240 Eastern Transvaal
South Africa   Profile no. 181

CAPE SCHOOL of MISSIONS
PO Box 17008 Ravensmead 7504
South Africa   Profile no.

EVANGELICAL BIBLE SEMINARY of SOUTH AFRICA
PO Box 2400 Pietermaritzburg 3200
South Africa   Profile no. 182

OPERATION MOBILISATION TRAINING CENTRE
PO Box 30221, Sunnyside, Pretoria 0132
South Africa   Profile no. 183

ROSEBANK BIBLE COLLEGE
PO Box 52047, Saxonwold 2132
South Africa   Profile no. 184

PROJECTO MAGREB, Curso de Orientacion Transcultural
Apdo 573 Granada 18080
Spain   Profile no. 185

LANKA BIBLE COLLEGE
PO Box 2 Peradeniya
Sri Lanka   Profile no. 186

SWAZILAND EVANGELICAL BIBLE INSTITUTE
Box 249 Mbabane
Swaziland   Profile no.

LIDINGO THEOLOGICAL SEMINARY
Kottlavagen 116, S - 181 41 Lidingo
Sweden   Profile no.

MISSIONSSKOLA och BIBELINSTITUT, Swedish Alliance Mission
S-55594 Jonköping
Sweden   Profile no. 187

ÖREBRO THEOLOGICAL SEMINARY, The Mission Institute
Box 1623, S - 701 16 Örebro
Sweden   Profile no. 188

Bibelheim und Bibelschule BEATENBERG
CH - 3803 Beatenberg
Switzerland   Profile no.

CHRISCHONA BIBELSCHULE
4126 Bettingen, Basel
Switzerland   Profile no.

EMMAUS Institut Biblique et Missionaire
Route de Fenil, 1806 St Legier
Switzerland　　　　　　　　　　　　　　　　　**Profile no.**

UNIVERSITY of the NATIONS (YWAM), Lausanne Center
1000 Lausanne 25
Switzerland　　　　　　　　　　　　　　　　　**Profile no. 189**

CHUO CHA BIBLIA NANJOKA
S L P 34 Tunduru
Tanzania　　　　　　　　　　　　　　　　　**Profile no.**

SCHOOL OF FRONTIER MISSIONS (YWAM)
Private Bag 62 Nuku'alofa
Tonga　　　　　　　　　　　　　　　　　**Profile no.**

TONGA BIBLE COLLEGE
PO Box 2462 Nuku'alofa
Tonga　　　　　　　　　　　　　　　　　**Profile no. 190**

WEST INDIES SCHOOL of THEOLOGY
#4 Bridge, Maracas Valley, Curepe
Trinidad　　　　　　　　　　　　　　　　　**Profile no.**

BISHOP TUCKER THEOLOGICAL COLLEGE
PO Box 4, Mukono
Uganda　　　　　　　　　　　　　　　　　**Profile no.**

DONETSK BIBLE COLLEGE
106-a Ilyitcha Prospekt, Donetsk
Ukraine　　　　　　　　　　　　　　　　　**Profile no. 191**

ALL NATIONS CHRISTIAN COLLEGE
Easneye, Ware, Herts. SG12 8LX, ENGLAND
United Kingdom　　　　　　　　　　　　　　**Profile no. 192**

BELFAST BIBLE COLLEGE, Glenburn House, Glenburn Road South,
Dunmurry, Belfast   BT17 9JP   NORTHERN IRELAND
United Kingdom　　　　　　　　　　　　　　**Profile no. 193**

BIRMINGHAM BIBLE INSTITUTE
5 Pakenham Rd., Edgbaston, Birmingham B15 2NN ENGLAND
United Kingdom　　　　　　　　　　　　　　**Profile no. 194**

CAREY COLLEGE
PO Box 1002 Bawtry, Doncaster, S Yorkshire DN10 6SP ENGLAND
United Kingdom　　　　　　　　　　　　　　**Profile no. 195**

CONWY HOUSE TRAINING CENTRE
115 Russell Road, Rhyl, Clwyd LL18 4ED WALES
United Kingdom   **Profile no. 196**

CROWTHER HALL
Weoley Park Rd, Selly Oak, Birmingham   B29 6QT ENGLAND
United Kingdom   **Profile no. 197**

ELIM BIBLE COLLEGE
1,The Grove, London Road, Nantwich, Cheshire CW5 6LW
United Kingdom   **Profile no. 198**

EMMANUEL BIBLE COLLEGE
1 Palm Grove, Birkenhead, Merseyside L43 1TE ENGLAND
United Kingdom   **Profile no. 199**

EQUIP, Bawtry Hall
Bawtry, Doncaster DN10 6JH   ENGLAND
United Kingdom   **Profile no. 200**

EVANGELICAL THEOLOGICAL COLLEGE of WALES
Bryntirion House, Bridgend Mid-Glam. CF31 4DX WALES
United Kingdom   **Profile no. 201**

GLASGOW BIBLE COLLEGE
731 Great Western Road, Glasgow G12 8QX SCOTLAND
United Kingdom   **Profile no. 202**

LUKE TRAINING CENTRE - OPERATION MOBILISATION
Zion, Little Cornbow, Halesowen, W.Midlands B63 3AJ ENGLAND
United Kingdom   **Profile no. 203**

MOORLANDS COLLEGE
Sopley, Christchurch, Dorset BH23 7AT ENGLAND
United Kingdom   **Profile no. 204**

NORTHUMBRIA BIBLE COLLEGE
52 Castle Terrace, Berwick- upon-Tweed TD15 1PA ENGLAND
United Kingdom   **Profile no. 205**

OVERSEAS COUNCIL for THEOLOGICAL EDUCATION & MISSION
49 High Street, Thornbury, Avon BS12 ENGLAND
United Kingdom   **Profile no.**

OXFORD CENTRE for MISSION STUDIES
PO Box 70 Oxford OX2 6HB ENGLAND
United Kingdom   **Profile no. 206**

REDCLIFFE COLLEGE
Wotton House, Horton Road, Gloucester, Glos. GL1 ENGLAND
United Kingdom   **Profile no. 207**

SELLEY OAK COLLEGES, Department of Mission,
Weoley Park Rd, Selly Oak, Birmingham B29 6LQ, ENGLAND
United Kingdom   **Profile no. 208**

SOUTHALL SCHOOL of Languages & Missionary Orientation
Western Road, Southall, Middx. UB2 5DS ENGLAND
United Kingdom   **Profile no. 209**

ST JOHN'S COLLEGE, Extension Studies Department
Bramcote, Nottingham NG9 3DS ENGLAND
United Kingdom   **Profile no.**

SUMMER INSTITUTE of LINGUISTICS, British School
Horsleys Green, High Wycombe, Bucks. HP14 3XL ENGLAND
United Kingdom   **Profile no. 210**

THE MISSIONARY TRAINING SERVICE, Oswestry Christian Centre
Lower Brook Street, Oswestry, Shropshire SY11 2XY ENGLAND
United Kingdom   **Profile no. 211**

TRINITY COLLEGE
24 Stoke Hill, Bristol, Avon BS9 1JP ENGLAND
United Kingdom   **Profile no. 212**

TURNING POINT TRAINING CENTRE (OM)
134 Gordon Road, West Ealing, London W13 8PJ ENGLAND
United Kingdom   **Profile no. 213**

WEC INTERNATIONAL, Intl.Training & Resources Officer
Bulstrode, Oxford Road, Gerrards Cross, Bucks. SL9 8SZ ENGLAND
United Kingdom   **Profile no.**

YOUTH WITH A MISSION
13 Highfield Oval, Harpenden, Herts. AL5 4BX ENGLAND
United Kingdom   **Profile no.**

AABC
PO Box 1523 Fayetteville AR 72701
United States Of America   **Profile no.**

ABILENE CHRISTIAN UNIVERSITY
ACU Station Box 7939 Abilene TX 79699
United States Of America   **Profile no.**

ACTION INTERNATIONAL MINISTRIES
PO Box 490 Bothwell WA 98041
United States Of America Profile no.

AGAPE INTERNATIONAL TRAINING, , Campus Crusade
PO Box 10389 Bakersfield CA 93309
United States Of America Profile no. 214

ALASKA BIBLE COLLEGE
Box 289 Glennallen AK 99588
United States Of America Profile no. 215

AMERICAN CHRISTIAN THEOLOGICAL SEMINARY
247 Euclid Pl, Upland CA 91786
United States Of America Profile no.

AMOR MINISTRIES
1664 Precision Park Lane, San Diego CA 92115
United States Of America Profile no. 216

APPALACHIAN BIBLE COLLEGE
Bradley WV 25818
United States Of America Profile no.

ARIZONA COLLEGE of the BIBLE, Dept. of Cross-Cultural Studies
2045 W. Northern Avenue, Phoenix AZ 85021
United States Of America Profile no. 217

ASBURY THEOLOGICAL SEMINARY
2012 Hartford Ct., Lexington KY 40514
United States Of America Profile no.

ASBURY THEOLOGICAL SEMINARY, E. Stanley Jones School of
World Mission, 204 N. Lexington Avenue, Wilmore KY 40390
United States Of America Profile no.

ASHLAND THEOLOGICAL SEMINARY
582 Messiah Village, Mechanicsburg PA 17055
United States Of America Profile no.

ASIA PACIFIC BIBLE SCHOOLS REGIONAL OFFICE (APBSRO)
23232 Peralta Drive, Suite 212, Laguna Hills CA 92653
United States Of America Profile no.

ASSEMBLIES OF GOD, Division of Foreign Missions
1445 Boonville Avenue, Springfield MO 65802
United States Of America Profile no.

AZUSA PACIFIC UNIVERSITY, Global Studies Program
901 E. Alosta Avenue, Azusa CA   91702
United States Of America   Profile no. 218

BANGUI EVANGELICAL SCHOOL of THEOLOGY
6140 Loren Drive, Minneapolis MN 55417
United States Of America   Profile no.

BAPTIST BIBLE SEMINARY
538 Venard Road, Clarks Summit PA   18411
United States Of America   Profile no. 219

BAYLOR UNIVERSITY
Waco TX 76703
United States Of America   Profile no.

BELHAVEN COLLEGE
1500 Peachtree Street, Jackson MS   39202 - 1789
United States Of America   Profile no. 220

BETHANY COLLEGE OF MISSIONS
6820 Auto Club Road, Minneapolis MN   55438
United States Of America   Profile no. 221

BETHEL COLLEGE INDIANA
1001 W. McKinley Avenue, Mishawaka IN   46545
United States Of America   Profile no. 222

BIOLA UNIVERSITY, School of International Studies
13800 Biola Ave, La Mirada CA 90639
United States Of America   Profile no.

BRYAN COLLEGE
Bryan Hill, Dayton TX 37321
United States Of America   Profile no.

CALVIN MISSIONS INSTITUTE
3233 Burton Street S.E. Grand Rapids MI   49546
United States Of America   Profile no. 223

CALVIN THEOLOGICAL SEMINARY
7090 Eldred NE, Rockford MI 49341
United States Of America   Profile no.

CARVER BIBLE INSTITUTE
PO Box 4335 , Atlanta GA   30302
United States Of America   Profile no.

CASCADE BIBLE COLLEGE
13646 NE 24th Street, Bellevue WA   98005
United States Of America   **Profile no.**

CEDARVILLE COLLEGE
PO Box 601 Cedarville OH   45314
United States Of America   **Profile no. 224**

CENTRAL BAPTIST THEOLOGICAL SEMINARY
Seminary Heights, Kansas City KS   66112
United States Of America   **Profile no.**

CENTRAL BIBLE COLLEGE
3000 N Grant, Springfield MO 65803
United States Of America   **Profile no.**

CHRISTIAN HERITAGE COLLEGE, Tecate Mission
501 Anita Street #52, Chula Vista CA 92011
United States Of America   **Profile no.**

CHURCH OF GOD SCHOOL of THEOLOGY, Missiology Program
PO Box 3330 Cleveland TN   37320 - 3330
United States Of America   **Profile no. 225**

CINCINNATI BIBLE COLLEGE & SEMINARY
PO Box 043200 Cincinnati OH   45204 -3200
United States Of America   **Profile no.**

COLUMBIA INTERNATIONAL UNIVERSITY
PO Box 3122 Columbia SC 29230
United States Of America   **Profile no. 226**

CONCORDIA COLLEGE , Oswald Hoffman School of Outreach
275 N. Syndicate, St Paul MN   55104
United States Of America   **Profile no. 227**

CONCORDIA SEMINARY
801 Demun, St Louis MO   63105
United States Of America   **Profile no.**

COVENANT COLLEGE
Lookout Mountain TN 37350
United States Of America   **Profile no.**

DALLAS THEOLOGICAL SEMINARY, Department of World Missions
United States Of America   **Profile no. 228**

DENVER SEMINARY, Department of World Christianity
P O Box 10,000 Denver CO 80250
United States Of America　　　　　　　　　　　　　Profile no. 229

EASTERN COLLEGE, Economic Development
10 Fairview Drive, St. Davids PA 19087 - 3696
United States Of America　　　　　　　　　　　　　Profile no. 230

EMMAUS BIBLE COLLEGE
2570 Asbury Road, Dubuque IA 52001
United States Of America　　　　　　　　　　　　　Profile no. 231

ESCUELA DE MISIONES BETANIA
Calle 13 S. O. # 824, Caparra Terrace PR 00921
United States Of America　　　　　　　　　　　　　Profile no. 232

EUGENE BIBLE COLLEGE
2155 Bailey Hill Road, Eugene OR 97405
United States Of America　　　　　　　　　　　　　Profile no. 233

FAITH BAPTIST BIBLE COLLEGE & SEMINARY
Dept. of World Missions, 1900 N.W. 4th Street, Ankeny IA 50021
United States Of America　　　　　　　　　　　　　Profile no. 234

FAITH EVANGELICAL LUTHERAN SEMINARY
P O Box 7186 Tacoma WA 98407
United States Of America　　　　　　　　　　　　　Profile no. 235

FORT WAYNE BIBLE COLLEGE
1025 W Rudisill Blvd., Ft Wayne IN 46807
United States Of America　　　　　　　　　　　　　Profile no.

FREEWILL BAPTIST BIBLE COLLEGE
3606 West End Avenue, Nashville TN 37205
United States Of America　　　　　　　　　　　　　Profile no. 236

FULLER THEOLOGICAL SEMINARY, School of World Mission
135 N. Oakland Avenue, Pasadena CA 91182
United States Of America　　　　　　　　　　　　　Profile no. 237

GEORGE FOX COLLEGE, Department of Religious Studies
414 N. Meridian # 6024, Newberg OR 97132 - 2697
United States Of America　　　　　　　　　　　　　Profile no. 238

GORDON CONWELL THEOLOGICAL SEMINARY, Dept. of Missions
130 Essex Street, South Hamilton MA 01982
United States Of America　　　　　　　　　　　　　Profile no. 239

GRACE BIBLE COLLEGE
PO Box 910 Grand Rapids MI 49509
United States Of America   Profile no.

GRACE COLLEGE OF THE BIBLE, Intercultural Ministry Major
Ninth & William, Omaha NE 68108
United States Of America   Profile no. 240

GRAND CANYON UNIVERSITY
PO Box 11097 Phoenix AZ 85061
United States Of America   Profile no.

GRAND RAPIDS BAPTIST SEMINARY
100 East Beltline NE, Grand Rapids MI 49505
United States Of America   Profile no. 241

GRAND RAPIDS SCHOOL of BIBLE & MISSIONS
7034 Independence, Grand Rapids MI 49548
United States Of America   Profile no.

HARDING UNIVERSITY GRADUATE SCHOOL OF RELIGION
1000 Cherry Road, Memphis TN 38117
United States Of America   Profile no. 242

HOLMES COLLEGE of the BIBLE
115 Briggs Ave., Greenville SC 29601
United States Of America   Profile no.

HOUGHTON COLLEGE
Rt1 Box 4-A, Houghton NY 14744
United States Of America   Profile no.

HUNTINGTON COLLEGE
Huntington IN 46750
United States Of America   Profile no.

INSTITUTE FOR INTERNATIONAL CHRISTIAN
COMMUNICATION   IICC - PO Box 14519 Portland OR 97215
United States Of America   Profile no. 243

INTERACT Ministries
31000 SE Kelso Road, Boring OR 97009
United States Of America   Profile no.

INTERNATIONAL CENTER for URBAN TRAINING
PO Box 143 San Jose CA 95103
United States Of America   Profile no. 244

INTERNATIONAL TEAMS
PO Box 203 Prospect Heights IL 60070
United States Of America Profile no. 245

JOHN BROWN UNIVERSITY
3500 Sumac, Siloam Springs AR 72761
United States Of America Profile no.

JOHNSON BIBLE COLLEGE, Cross-cultural Ministries
7900 Johnson Drive, Knoxville TN 37998
United States Of America Profile no. 246

KENTUCKY CHRISTIAN COLLEGE
Grayson KY 41143
United States Of America Profile no.

KINGS COLLEGE
Briarcliff Manor NY 10510
United States Of America Profile no.

LANCASTER BIBLE COLLEGE
9001 Eden Road, Lancaster PA 17601
United States Of America Profile no. 247

LE TOURNEAU UNIVERSITY
PO Box 7001 Longview TX 75607
United States Of America Profile no.

LIBERTY BIBLE COLLEGE
PO Box 3138 Pensacola FL 34506
United States Of America Profile no.

LIFE BIBLE COLLEGE
5851 Columbus Ave, Van Nuys CA 91411
United States Of America Profile no.

LIFE BIBLE COLLEGE, World Mission Department
1100 W. Covina Blvd., San Dimas CA 91773
United States Of America Profile no. 248

LINCOLN CHRISTIAN COLLEGE & SEMINARY, World Missions Dept.
United States Of America Profile no. 249

LINK CARE CENTER
1734 W. Shaw Avenue, Fresno CA 93711
United States Of America Profile no. 250

LUTHERAN BIBLE INSTITUTE
4221 228th S.E., Issaquah WA 98027
United States Of America   **Profile no. 251**

LUTHERAN BRETHREN SCHOOL
RR4 Box 22A Fergus Falls MN 56537
United States Of America   **Profile no.**

MANHATTAN CHRISTIAN COLLEGE, Cross-cultural Ministries
1415 Anderson Avenue, Manhattan KS 66502
United States Of America   **Profile no. 252**

MENNONITE BRETHREN BIBLICAL SEMINARY
4824 E Butler, Fresno CA 93727
United States Of America   **Profile no.**

MID-AMERICA BAPTIST THEOLOGICAL SEMINARY
PO Box 3624 Memphis TN 38173-0624
United States Of America   **Profile no. 253**

MID-AMERICAN BAPTIST THEOLOGICAL COLLEGE
1255 Poplar, Memphis TN 38104
United States Of America   **Profile no.**

MISSIONARY INTERNSHIP
P O Box 50110 Colorado Springs, CO 80949
United States Of America   **Profile no. 254**

MOODY BIBLE INSTITUTE, Dept. of World Missions & Evangelism
820 N. La Salle Blvd., Chicago IL 60610-3284
United States Of America   **Profile no. 255**

MOODY GRADUATE SCHOOL, Moody Bible Institute
820 N La Salle Blvd., Chicago IL 60610
United States Of America   **Profile no.**

MULTNOMAH BIBLE COLLEGE
8435 NE Glisan Street, Portland OR 97220
United States Of America   **Profile no. 256**

MUSLIM WORLD INTERNSHIP INTERCULTURAL
EFFECTIVENESS
United States Of America   **Profile no. 257**

NAZARENE BIBLE COLLEGE
1529 Lyle Drive, Colorado Springs Co 80915
United States Of America   **Profile no.**

NAZARENE THEOLOGICAL SEMINARY
15539 W 146th Street, Olathe KS 66062
United States Of America Profile no.

NAZARENE THEOLOGICAL SEMINARY, School of World Mission
& Evangelism , 1700 E. Meyer Blvd., Kansas City MO 64131
United States Of America Profile no. 258

NEBRASKA CHRISTIAN COLLEGE
1800 Syracuse Avenue, Norfolk NE 68701
United States Of America Profile no. 259

NORTH AMERICAN BAPTIST SEMINARY
1321 West 22nd Street, Sioux Falls SD 57105
United States Of America Profile no. 260

NORTH PARK THEOLOGICAL SEMINARY
3225 W. Foster Avenue, Chicago IL 60625- 489 5
United States Of America Profile no. 261

NORTHEASTERN BIBLE COLLEGE
Essex Fells NJ 07021
United States Of America Profile no.

NORTHWESTERN COLLEGE
1850 W County Rd C-2, St Paul MN 55113
United States Of America Profile no.

NORTHWESTERN COLLEGE
3003 Snelling Avenue N, Roseville MN 55113.
United States Of America Profile no. 262

NORTHWESTERN COLLEGE of the ASSEMBLIES OF GOD
PO Box 579, Kirkland WA 98083- 0579
United States Of America Profile no.

OAK HILLS BIBLE COLLEGE, Intercultural Studies
1600 Oak Hills Rd. S.W. , Bemidji MN 56601-3034
United States Of America Profile no. 263

OKHLAHOMA BAPTIST UNIVERSITY
500 W. University, Shawnee OK 74801
United States Of America Profile no. 264

ORAL ROBERTS UNIVERSITY, School of Theology & Missions
7777 S. Lewis Avenue, Tulsa OK 74171
United States Of America Profile no. 265

OREGON BIBLE COLLEGE
PO Box 100 Oregon IL 61061
United States Of America   **Profile no.**

OZARK BIBLE COLLEGE
111 N Main, Joplin MO 64801
United States Of America   **Profile no.**

PACIFIC CHRISTIAN COLLEGE, Intercultural Studies Degree
2500 E Nutwood, Fullerton CA 92631
United States Of America   **Profile no. 266**

PHILADELPHIA COLLEGE of the BIBLE
Langhorne PA 19047
United States Of America   **Profile no.**

PIEDMONT BIBLE COLLEGE
716 Franklin St, Winston Salem NC 27101
United States Of America   **Profile no.**

PUGET SOUND CHRISTIAN COLLEGE
410 4th Ave N, Edmonds WA 98020
United States Of America   **Profile no.**

REFORMED BIBLE COLLEGE
3333 East Beltline, NE, Grand Rapids MI 49505
United States Of America   **Profile no.**

REFORMED THEOLOGICAL SEMINARY
117-B Crestwood Cove, Clinton MS 39056
United States Of America   **Profile no.**

REFORMED THEOLOGICAL SEMINARY
5422 Clinton Blvd., Jackson MS 39209 - 3099
United States Of America   **Profile no.**

REGENT UNIVERSITY, School of Divinity
1000 Centerville Turnpike, Virginia Beach VA 23464 - 5041
United States Of America   **Profile no. 267**

RIO GRANDE BIBLE INSTITUTE
4300 S. Business 281, Edinburgh TX 78539
United States Of America   **Profile no. 268**

ROANOKE BIBLE COLLEGE, Cross-cultural Studies Department
714 1st Street, Elizabeth City NC 27909
United States Of America   **Profile no. 269**

SCHOOL OF INTERCULTURAL STUDIES
P O Box 250 Union Mills NC 28167
United States Of America Profile no.

SEATTLE PACIFIC UNIVERSITY
3rd Ave W & Nickerson, Seattle WA 98114
United States Of America Profile no.

SEMINARIO BIBLICO MEDELLIN COLLEGE
784 Santa Barbara Street, Pasadena CA 91101
United States Of America Profile no.

SEMINARY OF THE EAST
275 Commerce Drive, Suite 314, Fort Washington PA 19034
United States Of America Profile no.

SOUTH WESTERN COLLEGE
PO Box 340 Bethany OK 73008
United States Of America Profile no.

SOUTHEASTERN BIBLE COLLEGE, Department of World Missions
3001 Highway 280 E., Birmingham AL 35243
United States Of America Profile no. 270

SOUTHERN CALIFORNIA COLLEGE
55 Fair Drive, Costa Mesa CA 92626
United States Of America Profile no.

SOUTHWESTERN BAPTIST THEOLOGICAL COLLEGE
12375 Oak Grove Rd S , Burleston TX 76028
United States Of America Profile no.

SUMMER INSTITUTE OF LINGUISTICS
7500 W. Camp Wisdom Road, Dallas TX 75236
United States Of America Profile no.

SUMMIT CHRISTIAN COLLEGE
1025 Rudisill, Fort Wayne In 46807- 2140
United States Of America Profile no.

TENNESSEE TEMPLE UNIVERSITY
1815 Union Avenue, Chattanooga TN 37404
United States Of America Profile no.

TOCCOA FALLS COLLEGE, School of World Missions
PO Box 800297 Toccoa Falls GA 30598
United States Of America Profile no. 271

TRINITY EVANGELICAL DIVINITY SCHOOL, School of World
Mission and Evangelism , 2065 Half Day Road, Deerfield IL 60015
United States Of America   **Profile no. 272**

U S CENTER for WORLD MISSION
1605 E. Elizabeth Street, Pasadena CA 91104
United States Of America   **Profile no.**

WASHINGTON BIBLE COLLEGE
6511 Princess Graden Pkwy, Lanham MD 20706
United States Of America   **Profile no.**

WESTERN BAPTIST COLLEGE
5000 Deer Park Drive SE, Salem OR 97301-9392
United States Of America   **Profile no. 273**

WESTERN EVANGELICAL SEMINARY
P O Box 23939 Portland OR 97281-3939
United States Of America   **Profile no.**

WESTERN SEMINARY, Division of Intercultural Studies
5511 SE Hawthornes Blvd., Portland OR 97215
United States Of America   **Profile no. 274**

WESTMINSTER THEOLOGICAL SEMINARY, Urban Missions
Program
United States Of America   **Profile no. 275**

WESTMONT COLLEGE
955 LaPaz Road , Santa Barbara CA 93108
United States Of America   **Profile no.**

WHEATON COLLEGE GRADUATE SCHOOL Missions Department
Wheaton IL 60187
United States Of America   **Profile no.**

WHEATON COLLEGE, Institute for Cross-cultural Training
812 N President, Wheaton IL 60187
United States Of America   **Profile no. 276**

WILLIAM CAREY INTERNATIONAL UNIVERSITY
1539 E. Howard Street, Pasadena CA 91104
United States Of America   **Profile no.**

WILLIAM TYNDALE COLLEGE
35700 W 12 Mile Road, Farmington MI 48018
United States Of America   **Profile no.**

WORLD INSTITUTE for CROSS- CULTURAL EVANGELISM
STUDIES   PO Box 4100 Cincinnati OH   45204-4100
United States Of America Profile no. 277

WORLD LINK UNIVERSITY
5511 S E Hawthorne Blvd., Portland OR   97215
United States Of America Profile no.

ZWEMER INSTITUTE for MUSLIM STUDIES
PO Box 41330 Pasadena CA   91114 - 8330
United States Of America Profile no.

TALUA MINISTRY TRAINING CENTRE
PO Box 242 Santo
Vanuatu Profile no. 278

CEMA
Cra. Cucuta Manz. 51 #5, Villa Colombia. Pto. Ordaz
Venezuela Profile no.

OPERACION TIMOTEO
c/o Depto de Capacitation, Apartado 16377 Caracas 1011-A
Venezuela, Profile no. 279

SEMINARIO EVANGELICO ASOCIADO
Apartado 2050 Maracay, Aragua 2101 A,
Venezuela, Profile no. 280

SEMINARIO EVANGELICO DE CARACAS
Apdo. 40070 Caracas
Venezuela Profile no.

ECOLE SUPERIEURE DE THEOLOGIE EVANGELIQUE
P O Box 6289 Lubumbashi 10, Region du Shaba
Zaire Profile no. 281

Part **THREE**

Profiles

of the 281 missionary training programs in the IMTF Network which completed the questionnaire.

*Note : The profiles are listed alphabetically by nation;
and then, within each nation, alphabetically by title.*

Profile no. 1   **Argentina**

Established 1946
INSTITUTO BIBLICO BUENOS AIRES

Mailing address   INSTITUTO BIBLICO BUENOS AIRES
La Pampa 2975
1428 Capital Federal ARGENTINA

                          Phone 54 - 783 1127   **Fax** 54 - 786 4404

Location   as above

Director of program   Dr. Steven Voth, Academic Dean

Teaching staff   25 Western - 6 with cross-cultural experience
0 non-Western

Languages of instruction   Spanish

Learning styles   90% formal class-room teaching
10% non-formal learning experiences

Courses offered   Missiology degree at master's level
World Mission courses in bachelor's degree
World Mission courses at certificate or diploma level

Training ethos   The Buenos Aires Bible Institute offers a program in foundational missiological courses which can be supplemented by courses in the fields of history, theology, applied theology and bible.

Advanced missiology courses are offered for those completing the foundational programs.

Profile no. 2 **Argentina**

Established 1977
INSTITUTO BIBLICO CORDOBA

Mailing address INSTITUTO BIBLICO CORDOBA
Esquiv´ 247 B° General Paz
5,000 Cordoba ARGENTINA

Phone 54 - 51 7170   **Fax** 54 - 51 3802

Location In the center of the country

Director of program Miguel Angel Franco

Teaching staff

Languages of instruction Spanish & English

Learning styles 60% formal class-room teaching
40% non-formal learning experiences

Courses offered World Mission courses in bachelor's degree

Training ethos Nuestra preparacion es elemental en el Programa de Misiones Mundiales. Our preparation is elemental in the World Mission Program.

Hay varios misioneros alrededor del mundo con nuestra preparacion. There are various missionaries around the world with our preparation.

Profile no. 3   Argentina

Established 1989
SCHOOL OF MISSIONS (YWAM)

Mailing address JUVENTUD CON UNA MISION (YWAM)
Casilla de Correo 595
1000 Correo Central
 Buenos Aires ARGENTINA

Phone 621 2480   **Fax**

Location as above

Director of program Shelley Leveridge

Teaching staff 1 Western - 1 with cross-cultural experience
6 non-Western - 6 with cross-cultural experience

Languages of instruction Spanish

Learning styles 40% formal class-room teaching
60% non-formal learning experiences

Courses offered World Mission courses at certificate or diploma level
Pre-field training & orientation - 1 year

Training ethos An intense training program designed to prepare and launch Latin Americans into ministry among the least reached.

Profile no. 4　　　　　　　　　　　　　　　　　　　Argentina

Established 1985
SEMINARIO EVANGELICO INTER-DENOMINACIONAL DE TEOLOGIA (SEIT)

Mailing address　SEMINARIO EVANGELICO INTERDENOMINACIONAL DE TEOLOGIA
Ave. Perón 1234. 1646 San Fernando
PCIA, Buenos Aires ARGENTINA

Phone 01-744 0645　　**Fax**

Location　as above

Director of program　Oswaldo Romano, Principal

Teaching staff　8 Western - 8 with cross-cultural experience
15 non-Western - 2 with cross-cultural experience

Languages of instruction　Spanish

Learning styles　80% formal class-room teaching
20% non-formal learning experiences

Courses offered　World Mission courses in bachelor's degree
World Mission courses at certificate or diploma level
Pre-field training & orientation
Post graduate course in missiology - 1 year

Training ethos　Degree & Diploma courses include a field trip to Indian villages in Paraguian jungle.

Courses are aimed at giving the potential missionary a sound biblical/theological basis together with a practical preparation in inculturalization, language learning, living in a different culture etc.

Profile no. 5   **Australia**

Established 1947
BIBLE COLLEGE OF QUEENSLAND

Mailing address   BIBLE COLLEGE of QUEENSLAND
1 Cross Street
Toowong Brisbane Q 4066 AUSTRALIA

Phone 61-7 870 8355   **Fax** 61-7 371 4002

Location   as above

Director of program   Dr Kenneth J Newton, Principal

Teaching staff   6 Western - 3 with cross-cultural experience
0 non-Western

Languages of instruction   English

Learning styles   85% formal class-room teaching
15% non-formal learning experiences

Courses offered   World Mission courses in bachelor's degree
World Mission courses at diploma or certificate level
Pre-field training & orientation courses - 1 year

Training ethos   BCQ is an interdenominational and evangelical college which was established to provide biblical and theological studies and training in spiritual growth. It currently has a full-time student body of around 100 with several students from overseas. Students come from a wide range of denominations and with many and varied educational and employment experiences. Some classes are held in the evenings to assist those who are unable to attend during the day.

For those preparing for Missions, BCQ offers -
1 Regular contact with people involved in missions (through weekly exposure to missionaries & mission representatives).
2 Opportunities for short-term missions experience including cross-cultural field work experience

Profile no. 6   Australia

Established 1924
BIBLE COLLEGE OF SOUTH AUSTRALIA

Mailing address BIBLE COLLEGE of SOUTH AUSTRALIA
176 Wattle Street
Malvern, SA 5061 AUSTRALIA

Phone 61- 8 272 0188   **Fax** 61- 8 373 4185

Location as above - 3 kms from the centre of Adelaide

Director of program Rev. Raymond Laird, Principal

Teaching staff 4 Western- 3 with cross-cultural experience
0 non-Western

Languages of instruction English

Learning styles 75% formal class-room teaching
25% non-formal learning experiences

Courses offered Courses on World Mission as part of a bachelor's degree
Courses on World Mission at certificate or diploma level

Training ethos The College unites a solid academic curriculum with a family atmosphere in which students are encouraged to pursue their destiny of conformity to the image of Christ and equip themselves for ministries in a variety of situations.

Profile no. 7   Australia

Established 1920
BIBLE COLLEGE OF VICTORIA

Mailing address   BIBLE COLLEGE of VICTORIA
Centre for World Mission
PO Box 380
Lilydale, Vic 3140 AUSTRALIA

Phone 61- 3   735 0011   **Fax** 61- 3   735 0721

Location   71-81 Albert Hill Road, Lilydale, Melbourne

Director of program   Rev. Dr David J Price, Principal

Teaching staff   12 Western- 7 with cross-cultural experience
0 non-Western

Languages of instruction   English

Learning styles

Courses offered   Missiology courses at doctoral level
Missiology courses at bachelor's level
Courses on World Mission as part of a bachelor's degree
Courses on World Mission at certificate or diploma level

Training ethos

Profile no. 8   Australia

Established 1959
EMMAUS BIBLE COLLEGE

Mailing address   EMMAUS BIBLE COLLEGE
PO Box 234
Epping, NSW 2121 AUSTRALIA

Phone 61- 3 876 4370   **Fax** 61- 3 876 4354

Location   25 Ray Road, Epping, New South Wales

Director of program   Dr Keith Graham, Principal

Teaching staff   16 Western - 4 with cross-cultural experience
0 non-Western

Languages of instruction   English

Learning styles   80% formal class-room teaching
20% non-formal learning experiences

Courses offered   Courses on World Mission as part of a bachelor's degree
Courses on World Mission at certificate or diploma level

Training ethos   The Emmaus various curricula for the Associate Diploma, Diploma and Bachelor of Theology programmes are designed to extend a student's knowledge, skills and competency in areas relevant to a student's future ministry.

The programmes provide a healthy balance between theory and practice.

Emmaus is actively concerned with the spiritual formation of students through chapels. advisors. spiritual emphasis week and individual practice of spiritual disciplines.

Profile no. 9   Australia

Established 1947
KINGSLEY COLLEGE

Mailing address KINGSLEY COLLEGE
PO Box 125
Glenroy, Vic 3046 AUSTRALIA

Phone 61- 3 350 6681   **Fax** 61- 3 350 5561

Location 21 South Street, Glenroy, Victoria

Director of program Dr David R Wilson, Principal

Teaching staff 4 Western - 4 with cross-cultural experience
0 non-Western

Languages of instruction English

Learning styles 75% formal class-room teaching
25% non-formal learning experiences

Courses offered Courses on World Mission as part of a bachelor's degree
Courses on World Mission at certificate or diploma level

Training ethos Emphasis on training for effective urban mission in cross-cultural situations at home and overseas.

Profile no. 10   Australia

Established
MORLING COLLEGE

Mailing address   MORLING COLLEGE
120 Herring Road
Eastwood, NSW 2777 AUSTRALIA

Phone 61-2 878 0201   **Fax** 61-2 878 2175

Location   as above

Director of program   Rev Dr V J Eldridge, Principal

Teaching staff   7.5 Western - 3 with cross-cultural experience
0 non-Western

Languages of instruction   English

Learning styles   80% formal class-room teaching
20% non-formal learning experiences

Courses offered   Missiology courses at doctoral level
Missiology courses at bachelor's level
Courses on World Mission as part of a bachelor's degree
Courses on World Mission at certificate or diploma level

Training ethos   Mission training is taken in the same institution as training for pastoral and other types of ministry.

The focus is on academic, spiritual and practical aspects of learning.

Profile no. 11   Australia

Established 1928
PERTH BIBLE COLLEGE

Mailing address PERTH BIBLE COLLEGE
Private Bag 3
Karrinyup, W.A. 6018 AUSTRALIA

Phone 61- 9 448 0055   **Fax** 61- 9 448 0487

Location 1 College Court, Karrinyup, Perth.

Director of program Dr Alan F Meers, Principal

Teaching staff 5 Western - 1 with cross-cultural experience
0 non-Western

Languages of instruction English

Learning styles 75% formal class-room teaching
25% non-formal learning experiences

Courses offered World Mission courses at diploma or certificate level

Training ethos Perth Bible College is registered with the Government to accept full-fee overseas students into the fully accredited Diploma in Ministry Course, in one of 4 majors (including cross-cultural ministry.)

The programme has three aims :
It provides students with a Biblical foundation for life;
Promotes a Biblical lifestyle; and
Prepares students for a Biblical ministry.

Our training is very "hands-on". Students are required to be involved in community life and team ministries. Family accommodation available.

Profile no. 12   Australia

Established 1950
SOUTH PACIFIC SUMMER INSTITUTE OF LINGUISTICS

Mailing address   SOUTH PACIFIC SUMMER INSTITUTE of
LINGUISTICS
Graham Road.
Kangaroo Ground, Vic 3097 AUSTRALIA

Phone 61-3 712 0336   **Fax** 61-3 712 2799

Location   as above
Also at Fareham House. Featherston. NEW ZEALAND

Director of program   Dr.Warren Glover, Principal

Teaching staff   14 Western - 14 with cross-cultural experience
0 non-Western

Languages of instruction   English

Learning styles   85% formal class-room teaching
15% non-formal learning experiences

Courses offered   Pre-field training & orientation courses- 12 to15 months

Training ethos   SPSIL prepares people for cross-cultural service by courses in anthropology and training across cultures, phonetics and language learning, grammar, phonology and computer skills.

Two tracks specialise in field linguistics (linguistic analysis, semantics and translation) and literacy (theory of reading and a practical approach to helping communities acquire literacy).

Profile no. 13   Australia

Established 1964
ST. ANDREWS HALL

Mailing address St. ANDREW'S HALL,
190 The Avenue
Parkville, Vic 3052 AUSTRALIA

Phone 61- 3 388 1663   **Fax** 61- 3 387 1372

Location as above

Director of program Rev. Colin Reed

Teaching staff 4 Western - 3 with cross-cultural experience
0 non-Western

Languages of instruction English

Learning styles 40% formal class-room teaching
60% non-formal learning experiences

Courses offered Pre-field training & orientation - 6 months

Training ethos St Andrew's Hall is the Church Missionary Society (Australia) Institute for Inter-Cultural Studies. It caters especially for Anglican missionaries from Australia and NZ.

The course is designed for missionary candidates who have completed professional or trade training and Bible or Theological College.

Profile no. 14   Australia

Established 1916
SYDNEY MISSIONARY & BIBLE COLLEGE

Mailing address   SYDNEY MISSIONARY & BIBLE COLLEGE
39 Badminton Road
Croydon, NSW 2132 AUSTRALIA

Phone 61- 2 747 4780   **Fax** 61- 2 747 5053

Location   as above

Director of program   Rev David A Cook, Principal

Teaching staff   10 Western - 5 with cross-cultural experience
0 non-Western

Languages of instruction   English

Learning styles   75% formal class-room teaching
25% non-formal learning experiences

Courses offered   Courses on World Mission as part of a bachelor's degree
Courses on World Mission at certificate or diploma level

Training ethos   SMBC is interdeminational in charachter and evangelical in doctrine: it unreservedly holds to the Bible as the inspired Word of God and believes that the priority in missionary training must be to enable its students to know and teach the Word of God and to order their lives according to its teaching.

Profile no. 15   Australia

Established 1959
TAHLEE BIBLE COLLEGE

Mailing address TAHLEE BIBLE COLLEGE
Karuah, NSW   2324 AUSTRALIA

Phone 61- 49 973007   **Fax** 61- 49 973272

Location   as above

Director of program   Rev Howard C. Green, Principal

Teaching staff   10 Western - 1 with cross-cultural experience
0 non-Western

Languages of instruction   English

Learning styles   70% formal class-room teaching
30% non-formal learning experiences

Courses offered   World Mission courses at diploma or certificate level

Training ethos   One two and three year courses -

BASIC AIM to enable Christians to stand on their own feet without undue reliance on external resources; to win, disciple and train others for Christ.

ULTIMATE AIM to equip people for mission amongst peoples overseas from Australia; amongst ethnic minorities and Anglo-Australians within Australia.

Special emphasis on the study of the actual text of Scripture and on "in-service" training in which gifts are discovered
and developed.

Assessment not primarily by written examination, but rather by a blend of examination, character development, and completing achievements.

Profile no. 16   Australia

Established 1956
WEC MISSIONARY TRAINING COLLEGE

Mailing address WEC MISSIONARY TRAINING COLLEGE
PO Box 21, St.Leonards
Launceston, Tas   7250 AUSTRALIA

Phone 61-3 391204   **Fax** 61-3 391047

Location 41 Station Road, St. Leonards, Tasmania

Director of program A. Donald Barns, Principal

Teaching staff 6 Western - 6 with cross-cultural experience
1 non-Western - 1 with cross-cultural experience

Languages of instruction English

Learning styles 60% formal class-room teaching
40% non-formal learning experiences

Courses offered World Mission courses at diploma or certificate level
Pre-field training & orientation courses- about 4 months

Training ethos A Christian community existing to orient, equip and train called people for God's mission to the world, especially among the unreached peoples.

This is achieved through the cultivation of biblical attitudes, acquiring of useful, relevant knowledge and the development of appropriate skills to produce cross-cultural communicators.

Profile no. 17   Austria

Established 1990
MISSIONARY TRAINING SCHOOL, CENTRAL EUROPEAN TEAMS (OM)

Mailing address MISSIONARY TRAINING SCHOOL,
Central European Teams (OM)
Postfach 61
A 1212 Vienna AUSTRIA

Phone 334 95134   **Fax** 334 95185

Location c/- Rekre-Zoul
37350 Olesnik 30. CZECH REPUBLIC

Director of program Graham Roberts, Co-ordinator

Teaching staff 5 Western - 3 with cross-cultural experience
0 non-Western - a number of visiting lecturers

Languages of instruction English

Learning styles 40% formal class-room teaching
60% non-formal learning experiences

Courses offered Pre-field training & orientation - 11 weeks

Training ethos Our training focuses upon learning together, as staff and participants live on site together, learning from one another in a multinational community, learning through formal teaching & training sessions related to personal development & field ministry followed by small group discussion, personal reflection & projects and learning through a variety of informal situations and practical field experience.

Profile no. 18   Belgium

Established 1979
EVANGELICAL THEOLOGICAL FACULTY, BIJBELINSTITUUT BELGIE

Mailing address EVANGELICAL THEOLOGICAL FACULTY
(Bijbelinstituut Belgie)
St. Jansbergsesteenweg 97
3001 Heverlee- Leuven BELGIUM

Phone 32- 16- 200 895   **Fax** 32- 16- 200 943

Location as above

Director of program Dr.Y. Vleugels

Teaching staff 25 Western - 11 with cross-cultural experience
0 non-Western

Languages of instruction English (for Doctoral), Dutch (for Masters)

Learning styles 90% formal class-room teaching
10% non-formal learning experiences

Courses offered Missiology degree at doctoral level
Missiology degree at master's level

Training ethos The ETF is committed to the ministry of building up the Body of Christ and effectively equipping its students for Christian service.

Situated at the heart of Europe and mindful of the potential entrusted to it, the ETF desires to have a growing impact for the cause of Christ in Europe and the world.

Profile no. 19   Belgium

Established 1919
INSTITUT BIBLIQUE BELGE

Mailing address INSTITUT BIBLIQUE BELGE
rue E. Vondervelde, 63
6041 Gosselies BELGIUM

Phone 32- 71 35 61 49   **Fax**

Location   as above

Director of program   Alain Lambot

Teaching staff   12 Western - 2 with cross-cultural experience
1 non-Western - with no cross-cultural experience

Languages of instruction French

Learning styles   90% formal class-room teaching
10% non-formal learning experiences

Courses offered   World Mission courses in bachelor's degree
World Mission courses at certificate or diploma level

Training ethos

Profile no. 20 **Benin Republic**

Established 1994
ECOLE DE MISSION INTERAFRICAINE AU BENIN (EMIAB)

Mailing address ECOLE DE MISSION INTERAFRICAINE AU BENIN (EMIAB)
B.P. 01 - 3285
Cotonou BENIN

Phone 229- 32 10 18   **Fax**

Location Sekandji via Cotonou

Director of program Ogigirigi Emilia Tenere, Co-ordinator

Teaching staff 2 Western - 2 with cross-cultural experience
17 non-Western - 7 with cross-cultural experience

Languages of instruction French mainly & some English

Learning styles 40% formal class-room teaching
60% non-formal learning experiences

Courses offered World Mission courses at certificate or diploma level
Pre-field training & orientation

Training ethos The programme lasts for 12 months with some courses (classroom) lasting for one or two or four weeks; each having a total lecture hours of 6 and a half daily.

They also take part in manual labour and a 3 months practical field work.

Profile no. 21 — Brazil

Established 1976
ANTIOCH BIBLE SCHOOL - MISSIONARY TRAINING COURSE

Mailing address ANTIOCH BIBLE SCHOOL
Missionary Training Course
CP 582
01059 - 970 São Paulo - SP BRASIL

Phone 55- 11- 498 1273 **Fax** 55- 11- 498 1272

Location Valley of Blessing
Rodovia Castelo Branco. Km 50

Director of program Décio de Azevedo, Director

Teaching staff 50% Western - all with cross-cultural experience
50% non-Western - all with cross-cultural experience

Languages of instruction Portuguese

Learning styles 60% formal class-room teaching
40% non-formal learning experiences

Courses offered Pre-field training & orientation courses

Training ethos This is a school with emphasis on prayer and on the spiritual life of the student.

Our aim is to train the whole person not just academically - but especially spiritually and emotionally.

We also want to have missionaries who will be prepared for any kind of work. For this reason they are put in various situations to learn.

Profile no. 22 Brazil

Established 1989
BAPTIST CENTER FOR MISSIONARY TRAINING

Mailing address BAPTIST CENTER for MISSIONARY TRAINING
Rua Senador Furtado, 56
Praça da Bandeira
Rio de Janeiro 20270-020 BRASIL

Phone 55-21 284 2241   **Fax** 55-21 284 2436

Location no official centre at the moment of writing

Director of program Pastor David Alan Brown, Director

Teaching staff 1 Western - 1 with cross-cultural experience
3 non-Western - 2 with cross-cultural experience

Languages of instruction Portuguese

Learning styles 70% formal class-room teaching
30% non-formal learning experiences

Courses offered World Mission courses in bachelor's degree
Pre-field training & orientation courses - 1 month

Training ethos Our correspondence course is just beginning, aimed at providing missiological information and training for all who are interested - Pastors, Leaders, Vocationed.

Our residential course is only for those commissioned by the World Mission Board of the Brazilian Baptist Convention.

Profile no. 23   Brazil

Established 1984
CENTRE FOR THE NATIONS

Mailing address CENTRE FOR THE NATIONS
Caixa Postal 293
São Caetano do Sul, SP 09501-970 BRASIL

Phone 55-11 453 9795   **Fax** 55-11 453 9795

Location Monte Verde- Camanducáia, MG

Director of program Pastor David Botelho

Teaching staff 8Western - 8 with cross-cultural experience
0 non-Western

Languages of instruction Portuguese

Learning styles 60% formal class-room teaching
40% non-formal learning experiences

Courses offered World Mission courses at certificate or diploma level

Training ethos World Horizons is a multi-national ministry with a major focus on the Muslim world and the most unreached of Africa.

Our desire is to facilitate those who are being called. Consequently our introductory training focusses on developing the call and preparing the student to face the challemges of their future field.

We are not so much concerned with academic ability as practical and personal preparation for ministry; believing the Lord will take whoever makes himself available and reveal what is necesssarey in further training for ministry, as his initial field assignment proceeds.

Profile no. 24 **Brazil**

Established 1982
CENTRO DE TREINAMENTO MISSIONARIO BETANIA

Mailing address CENTRO de TREINAMENTO MISSIONARIO BETANIA
Caixa Postal 174
96180-000 Camaquã, RS BRASIL

Phone 55-51 671 3041   **Fax** 55-51 671 3041

Location 4 Distrito Galpões
96180-000 Camaquã, RS

Director of program Pastor Jessé H. Araújo

Teaching staff 9 Western - 2 with cross-cultural experience
0 non-Western

Languages of instruction Portuguese

Learning styles 70% formal class-room teaching
30% non-formal learning experiences

Courses offered World Mission courses at certificate or diploma level
Pre-field training & orientation courses -

Training ethos This is a theological course dealing in the areas of transcultural missions, pastoral training (church planting, discipleship, evangelism, etc.) and Christian education.

The length of the course is four years, including a one-year internship.

Profile no. 25   **Brazil**

Established 1984

CENTRO DE TREINAMENTO MISSIONARIO OF THE CHURCH OF GOD

Mailing address   CENTRO de TREINAMENTO MISSIONARIO of the
Church of God
Caixa Postal 14.139
São Paulo, SP 02731-000 BRASIL

Phone 55-11 875 3320   **Fax** 55-11 875 3320

Location   Praca Santa Marcela, 53
Freguesia do O. SP

Director of program   John T. Hayes, Director

Teaching staff   3 Western - 3 with cross-cultural experience
5 non-Western - 5 with cross-cultural experience

Languages of instruction   Portuguese, Spanish & English

Learning styles   50% formal class-room teaching
50% non-formal learning experiences

Courses offered   Pre-field training & orientation - 3 months to two years

Training ethos   Three month, six month and one year training programs are provided to train future missionary candidates in cross-cultural ministry.

Training involves academic training with experienced and recognized missiologists, as well as character formation and practical experience in cross-cultural ministry within the many ethnic groups of Sao Paulo.

Students are from all over South America as well as from the United States and Africa.

The instruction is from a Pentecostal perspective.

Profile no. 26   **Brazil**

Established 1989
CENTRO DE TREINAMENTO MISSIONARIO - OPERATION MOBILISATION

Mailing address   CENTRO DE TREINAMENTO MISSIONARIO
Av. Andromeda, 3621
Bosque dos Eucauptus
S.J. de Campos, SP 12233-000 BRASIL

                 Phone 55-242 42 1949   **Fax** 55-242 42 1949

Location   R. Paulo Buarque 497, Pque S. Vicente
25650-590 Petropolis. Rio de Janeiro

Director of program   Paulo Elias, Training Director

Teaching staff

Languages of instruction   Portuguese & Spanish

Learning styles   50% formal class-room teaching
50% non-formal learning experiences

Courses offered   World Mission courses at certificate or diploma level
Pre-field training & orientation - 1 year

Training ethos   Giving an exposure for the students of what cross-cultural involvement means in a short period term.

To have them exposed for planting churches, ministries, discipleship etc.

Profile no. 27   Brazil

Established 1983
CENTRO EVANGELICO DE MISSOES

Mailing address   CENTRO EVANGÉLICO de MISSOES
Caixa Postal 53
Viçosa, MG 36570-000 BRASIL

Phone 55-31 891 3030   **Fax** 55-31 891 3030

Location   Rod. Viçosa - Coimbra S/N
36570-000 Vicosa. MG

Director of program   Professor Carlos Del Pino

Teaching staff   10 Western - 7with cross-cultural experience
0 non-Western

Languages of instruction   Portuguese

Learning styles   70% formal class-room teaching
30% non-formal learning experiences

Courses offered   Missiology degree at master's level
World Mission courses at diploma or certificate level

Training ethos   CROSS-CULTURAL MINISTRY COURSE:
This undergraduate program equips university students and professionals with ctoss-cultural communication skills for tent-makers.

POST-GRADUATION PROGRAM:
(Specialization - "lato sensu" and Master in Missiology "stricto sensv"): equips pastors for cross-cultural planting and professors of Mission for teaching.

Profile no. 28   Brazil

Established 1965
INSTITUTO TEOLOGIA QUADRANGULAR

Mailing address   INSTITUTO TEOLOGIA QUADRANGULAR
Rua São Francisco - 204 - Centro
Curitiba, PR   80020-190 BRASIL

Phone 55-41 225 7491   **Fax**

Location   at downtown of Curitiba, PR

Director of program   Rev Marco Antonio T. Lapa

Teaching staff   0 Western
1 non-Western - with cross-cultural experience

Languages of instruction   Portuguese

Learning styles   75% formal class-room teaching
25% non-formal learning experiences

Courses offered   Pre-field training & orientation

Training ethos   Missiology was introduced in 1986 as a one year course.

During the sourse we study:
1)   A brief vision of missions history
2)   Biblical bases of missions
3)   The local church and missions
4)   The missionary
5)   Urban missions
6)   Cross cultural missions

Learning experience - work in one project to plant a church in one field that the various groups choose. We have groups of 10 students for placement.

We want to give students a view of mission, to really open this vision. Our Seminary prepares pastors and future pastors. When someone wants to go into missions we send them to our mission agency.

Profile no. 29   **Brazil**

Established 1989
KAIROS - ASS. PARA TREINAMENTO TRANSCULTURAL

Mailing address   KAIROS - ASS. PARA TREINAMENTO TRANSCULTURAL
Rua Angelo De Lucia. 228. Santo Amaro
São Paulo, SP   04756-000 BRASIL

Phone 55-11 246 5908   **Fax** 55-11 246 5908

Location   as above

Director of program   Pastor Waldemar Carvalho

Teaching staff   6 Western - 6 with cross-cultural experience
11 non-Western - 6 with cross-cultural experience

Languages of instruction   Portuguese

Learning styles   33%   formal class-room teaching
67%   non-formal learning experiences

Courses offered   Pre-field training & orientation - 9 months

Training ethos   KAIROS offers basic cross-cultural training in Brazil and specific field training in Peru, Colombia and North Africa.

Profile no. 30   Brazil

Established 1984
MTC LATINO AMERICANO

Mailing address MTC LATINO AMERICANO
Caixa Postal 289
Montes Claros, MG 39400-970 BRASIL

Phone 55-38 221 0790   **Fax** 55-38 221 4922

Location Sitio Aguas Vivas - Corredor do Pequi S/No
Vila Oliveira. Montes Claros. MG

Director of program Jose Rosifran Cruz Macedo, Director

Teaching staff 6 Western - 6 with cross-cultural experience
7 non-Western - 2 with cross-cultural experience

Languages of instruction Portuguese

Learning styles 50% formal class-room teaching
50% non-formal learning experiences

Courses offered World Mission courses in bachelor's degree
World Mission courses at certificate or diploma level

Training ethos We see ourselves as co-workers with Christ in the formation of mature disciples.

This maturity should be evidenced in an attitude of learning from God, information and circumstances.

Special attention is given to capacitating them for cross-cultural work.

Profile no. 31   Brazil

Established 1983
SAO PAULO BAPTIST THEOLOGICAL COLLEGE

Mailing address   FACULDADE TEOLOGICA BATISTA DE
SAO PAULO
Caixa Postal 70521
São Paulo, SP   05013- 990   BRASIL

Phone 55-11   652 148   **Fax** 55-11   262 6437

Location   Rua João Ramalho, 466 Perdizes
São Paulo. SP

Director of program   Donald E Price, Chair

Teaching staff   4Western - 4 with cross-cultural experience
3 non-Western - 2 with cross-cultural experience

Languages of instruction   Portuguese

Learning styles   70% formal class-room teaching
30% non-formal learning experiences

Courses offered   Missiology degree at master's level
World Mission courses in bachelor's degree
World Mission courses at certificate or diploma level

Training ethos   From 1983 we are training missionaries in the context of theological studies to assure a biblical basis for missions and to influence other students for missions in their churches and personal decisions for ministry.

We are attempting to serve the greater Sao Paulo area by offering our courses on missions in a concentrated manner - one semester per year, so that students or graduates from other schools can attend.

We desire to create a non-formal environment even in a formal school setting - each class being a dynamic interaction leading to practical application.

We seek to integrate classroom learning with practical experience.

Profile no. 32   Brazil

Established 1993
SCHOOL OF FRONTIER MISSIONS (YWAM)

Mailing address   JOVENS COM UNA MISSAO - School of Frontier Missions
Caixa Postal 524
Belo Horizonte, MG 30161-970 BRASIL

Phone 55-31 398 1488   **Fax** 55-31 398 1166

Location   as above

Director of program   Gilberto de Mello, Director

Teaching staff   2 Western - 2 with cross-cultural experience
2 non-Western - 2 with cross-cultural experience

Languages of instruction   Portuguese & English

Learning styles   60% formal class-room teaching
40% non-formal learning experiences

Courses offered   World Mission courses at certificate or diploma level
Pre-field training & orientation - 3 months

Training ethos   We understand that formal classroom learning is beneficial, but must be balanced with practical experience.

Our desire is to give the student a realistic view of his/her life on the mission field and what will await him/her therein.

Profile no. 33   Brazil

Established 1967
SEMINARIO E INSTITUTO BIBLICO BETANIA

Mailing address SEMINARIO e INSTITUTO BIBLICO BETANIA
Caixa Postal 10
Altônia, PR 87550-000 BRASIL

Phone 55-446 59 1220   **Fax** 55-446 59 1220

Location as above

Director of program Ccicero M. Bezerra, Director

Teaching staff 1 Western - 1 with cross-cultural experience
10 non-Western - 6 with cross-cultural experience

Languages of instruction Portuguese

Learning styles 60% formal class-room teaching
40% non-formal learning experiences

Courses offered World Mission courses at certificate or diploma level
Pre-field training & orientation courses

Training ethos Bible School program with strong emphasis on the character and training of pastors, miissionaries, social workers and the ministry of women in the church.

Profile no. 34　　　　　　　　　　　　　　　　　　　　　　**Brazil**

Established
SEMINARIO EVANGELICO BETANIA

Mailing address　SEMINARIO EVANGELICO BETANIA
Av. Tancredo Neves, 536
Cel. Fabriciano, MG 35170-074 BRASIL

Phone 55-31 842 1029　　　**Fax** 55-31 842 1274

Location　as above

Director of program　Joseph Palmer, Director

Teaching staff　4 Western - 4 with cross-cultural experience
9 non-Western - 0 with cross-cultural experience

Languages of instruction　Portuguese

Learning styles　50% formal class-room teaching
50% non-formal learning experiences

Courses offered　World Mission courses at certificate or diploma level

Training ethos　Our goal is to train Brazilians to be pastors and missionaries. We feel pastors should have a heart for missions and missionaries should have a pastor's heart.

Therefore, the course is the same for all our students. It is a 4year program with the 3rd year being an internship with either a church or a mission.

Profile no. 35   Brazil

Established 1977
SEMINARIO JOVENS DA VERDADE

Mailing address SEMINARIO JOVENS DA VERDADE
Caixa Postal 66
Aruja, SP   07400-970 BRASIL

Phone 55-11 466 1920   **Fax**

Location   Estrada dos Fernandes, Km 4 Mirante
Aruiá. São Paulo

Director of program   Ivone Lima Ferreira Botelho, Director

Teaching staff   3 Western - 3 with cross-cultural experience
14 non-Western - none with cross-cultural experience

Languages of instruction   Portuguese

Learning styles   60% formal class-room teaching
40% non-formal learning experiences

Courses offered   World Mission courses in bachelor's degree

Training ethos   The school offers a fulltime residential course with the numbers of students being limited in order to enable the leaders to accompany the progress of each student.

Basically the course provides lectures in the morning, sports and maintenance work in the afternoons and individual study in the evening. On Wednesday afternoons there is evangelism in schools, hospitals and the local prison.

Each student is allocated to a specific church for weekend ministry in July and in January the students are involved in pioneer work, camps, evangelistic campaigns etc. Thus when the student obtains his/her bachelors degree he/she already has completed 8 months experience in various types of work, orientated and supervised by a local church.

Profile no. 36   Brazil

Established
SEMINARIO TEOLOGICO BATISTA INDEPENDENTE

Mailing address SEMINARIO TEOLOGICO BATISTA INDEPENDENTE -
Curso de Missoes
Caixa Postal 1316
Campinas, SP 13001-970 BRASIL

Phone 55-192 520708   **Fax** 55-192 541346

Location as above

Director of program Bertil Ekstrom, Co-ordinator

Teaching staff 2 Western - 2 with cross-cultural experience
5 non-Western - 1 with cross-cultural experience

Languages of instruction Portuguese

Learning styles 70% formal class-room teaching
30% non-formal learning experiences

Courses offered World Mission courses in bachelor's degree
Pre-field training & orientation

Training ethos We believe that the local church is the basis for world mission and that even local pastors need missiological training.

The school belongs to a Baptist Convention (Batista Independente) and tries to give a good training and pre-field orientation to the new missionaries.

The courses are open to students from other denominations.

Profile no. 37 Brazil

Established 1986
SEMINARIO TEOLOGICO DE GRAMADO

Mailing address SEMINARIO TEOLOGICO DE GRAMADO
Caixa Postal 80
Gramado, RS   95670-000 BRASIL

Phone 55-54 286 1006   **Fax** 55-54 286 3170

Location Rua São Pedro, 1191

Director of program Heinrich Finger, Director

Teaching staff 6 Western - 6 with cross-cultural experience
15 non-Western - 5 with cross-cultural experience

Languages of instruction Portuguese

Learning styles 65% formal class-room teaching
35% non-formal learning experiences

Courses offered World Mission courses in bachelor's degree

Training ethos We have a bachelor in missions as well as a missions major.

Our emphasis is the student's development in three areas : academic, ministry (practical) & personal life.

Our program involves 4 years of residence training (including weekend ministry) plus a one year internship.

Profile no. 38 Brazil

Established 1987
SEMINARIO TEOLOGICO EVANGELICO BETEL BRASILEIRO

Mailing address SEMINARIO TEOLOGICO EVANGELICO
BETEL BRASILEIRO
Caixa Postal 8381
São Paulo, SP 01065-970 BRASIL

Phone 55-11 37 9518   **Fax** 55-11 885 2583

Location Rua São Bento, 545 - 2nd Sobreloja - Centro

Director of program Durvalina B. Bezerra, Director

Teaching staff 0 Western
21 non-Western - 4 with cross-cultural experience

Languages of instruction Portuguese

Learning styles 70% formal class-room teaching
30% non-formal learning experiences

Courses offered World Mission courses in bachelor's degree

Training ethos Our aims: to prepare disciples of Jesus who can serve the Lord wherever He sends them.

Our priority - missionary challenge national and foriegn mission.

Our program - thelogy and missiology as our prospectus can show you.

Profile no. 39 Brazil

Established 1980
SEMINARIO TEOLOGICO EVANGELICO PENIEL

Mailing address SEMINARIO TEOLOGICO EVANGELICO PENIEL
Av. Maracana, 63 - Maracana
Rio De Janeiro, RJ   20271-110 BRASIL

Phone 55-21 254 9492   **Fax**

Location as above

Director of program Adriano Augusto Magalhaes. Diretor-Geral

Teaching staff

Languages of instruction Portuguese

Learning styles 80% formal class-room teaching
20% non-formal learning experiences

Courses offered World Mission courses at certificate or diploma level

Training ethos The STEP missionary training course wants theological and practical formation of Christian students that have two or more years working on church activities .

We have prospectus to send.

Profile no. 40　　　　　　　　　　　　　　　　　　Brazil

Established 1965
WORD OF LIFE BIBLE SEMINARY

Mailing address　SEMINARIO BIBLICO PALAVRA da VIDA
Word of Life Bible Seminary
Caixa Postal 43
Atibaia, SP 12940-000 BRASIL

Phone 55-11 487 1377　　**Fax** 55-11 484 3716

Location　Estância Palavra da Vida
Atibaia. SP

Director of program　Carlos Osvaldo C. Pinto

Teaching staff　16 Western - 8 with cross-cultural experience
0 non-Western

Languages of instruction

Learning styles　90% formal class-room teaching
10% non-formal learning experiences

Courses offered　World Mission courses in bachelor's degree
World Mission courses at certificate or diploma level

Training ethos　We are a full-time school with an emphasis on Christian life and ministry, in a context of small-group orientation and discipleship.

Profile no. 41   Cameroon

Established 1990
MISSIONARY CENTER

Mailing address MISSIONARY CENTER
B.P. 6295 New-Bell
Douala CAMEROON

Phone 237- 40 02 13   **Fax**

Location as above

Director of program Djob Yogo Joseph

Teaching staff

Languages of instruction English & French

Learning styles 40% formal class-room teaching
60% non-formal learning experiences

Courses offered World Mission courses in bachelor's degree
World Mission courses at certificate or diploma level
Pre-field training & orientation -

Training ethos Our center trains missionaries following a program according to the vision of the Lord which follows.

Fundamental doctrine; Pastoral ministry; the Bible and its interpretation; Study of religions and traditions; evangelisation; ministry with married couples; cells of prayer; evangelisation in prison & in hospitals; financial administration; deacons' ministry; mass media; pastoral office; ministry with children; public relations; missiology.

Profile no. 42   Canada

Established
ACADIA DIVINITY COLLEGE

Mailing address ACADIA DIVINITY COLLEGE
Wolfville
Nova Scotia B0P 1X0 CANADA

Phone 902 - 542 2285   **Fax** 902 - 542 7527

Location as above

Director of program Dr H Miriam Ross

Teaching staff 1 Western - 1 with cross-cultural experience
0 non-Western

Languages of instruction English

Learning styles 100% formal class-room teaching
nil non-formal learning experiences

Courses offered Courses on world mission required in M Div program

Training ethos Introductory course (Biblical mandate, history of mission, contemporary world, mission methods, mission education in local church) required of students in Master of Divinity programme for missionary candidates and ministerial students some of whom come from overseas.

Other relevant mission courses taught as electives.

Profile no. 43   Canada

Established 1935
BRIERCREST BIBLE COLLEGE

Mailing address   BRIERCREST BIBLE COLLEGE
Intercultural Studies Department
510 College Drive
Caronport SK S0H 0S0 CANADA

Phone 306 - 756 3200   **Fax** 306 - 756 3366

Location   as above

Director of program   Rev. Robert Ratzliff

Teaching staff   2 Western - 2 with cross-cultural experience
0 non-Western

Languages of instruction   English

Learning styles   90% formal class-room teaching
10% non-formal learning experiences

Courses offered   World Mission courses in bachelor's degree
World Mission courses at certificate or diploma level

Training ethos   Our program is now called the Inter Cultural Studies Department.

It includes courses such as Missions/Evangelism, Cross cultural Communication, Cultural anthropology, World religions, Missions syntheses, Missions in the local church, Urban sociology, Missions principles etc.

Profile no. 44   Canada

Established 1988
CANADIAN BAPTIST SEMINARY

Mailing address   CANADIAN BAPTIST SEMINARY
7600 Glover Road
Langley, BC   V3A 6H4 CANADA

Phone 604 - 888 1265   **Fax** 604 - 888 1905

Location   as above

Director of program   Dr. Barrie J. Palfreyman, President

Teaching staff   3 Western - 1 with cross-cultural experience
0 non-Western

Languages of instruction   English

Learning styles   50% formal class-room teaching
50% non-formal learning experiences

Courses offered   Missiology degree at master's level

Training ethos   An applied, mentoring leadership graduate school with priorities in urban ministry and global missions, learning through classroom learning and internship.

Profile no. 45 — Canada

Established 1970
CANADIAN THEOLOGICAL SEMINARY

Mailing address CANADIAN THEOLOGICAL SEMINARY
4400 Fourth Ave
Regina, SK   S4T 0H8 CANADA

Phone 306 - 545 1515   **Fax** 306 - 545 0210

Location as above

Director of program Dr. Gordon Smith, Acad. Vice-President

Teaching staff 12 Western - 5 with cross-cultural experience
0 non-Western

Languages of instruction English

Learning styles 80% formal class-room teaching
20% non-formal learning experiences

Courses offered Missiology degree at doctoral level
Missiology degree at master's level

Training ethos Emphasis placed on training students for missionary service with the Christian & Missionary Alliance.

Full-time missionary-in-residence. Missions professor has extensive experience on the field. Adjunct professors of missiology & anthropology also on site.

Profile no. 46　　　　　　　　　　　　　　　　　　　　　　　　　Canada

Established 1989
NORTHWEST BAPTIST COLLEGE

Mailing address　NORTHWEST BAPTIST COLLEGE
P O Box 790
Langley BC　V3A 8B8　CANADA

　　　　　　　　　Phone　604 - 888 3310　　　**Fax**　604 - 888 3354

Location　　as above

Director of program　Dr Vern Middleton

Teaching staff　7 Western - 2 with cross-cultural experience
1 non-Western with cross-cultural experience

Languages of instruction　English

Learning styles　60% formal class-room teaching
40% non-formal learning experiences

Courses offered　Missiology degree at master's level
World Mission courses in bachelor's degree
World Mission courses at certificate or diploma level
Pre-field training & orientation - 2 semesters

Training ethos　Northwest Baptist College is an affiliate school of ACTS.

We send out mission teams to 4 or 5 countries each year.

Courses on World Religions are unique because of hands on exposure to the five major religions.

Profile no. 47 Canada

Established 1982
ONTARIO BIBLE COLLEGE

Mailing address ONTARIO BIBLE COLLEGE, Intercultural Studies
25 Ballyconnor Ct.
North York, Ont M2M 4B3 CANADA

Phone 416 - 226 6380   **Fax** 416 - 226 6746

Location as above

Director of program Dr. Ebenezer Sikakane

Teaching staff adjunct professors
1 non-Western - with cross-cultural experience

Languages of instruction English

Learning styles 85% formal class-room teaching
15% non-formal learning experiences

Courses offered World Mission courses in bachelor's degree

Training ethos The student who successfully completes the intercultural focus will be equipped to minister cross-culturally at home and abroad.

Students will be trained to function in diverse settings and situations often expected of a missionary in less "specialist-oriented" societies.

Profile no. 48   Canada

Established 1982
ONTARIO THEOLOGICAL SEMINARY

Mailing address ONTARIO THEOLOGICAL SEMINARY
Intercultural Focus
25 Ballvconnor Court
North York, ONT M2M 4B3 CANADA

Phone 416 - 226 6380   **Fax** 416 - 226 9464

Location as above

Director of program Dr. Irving A Whitt, Chair of Dept.

Teaching staff 14 Western - 9 with cross-cultural experience
2 non-Western with cross-cultural experience

Languages of instruction English

Learning styles 90% formal class-room teaching
10% non-formal learning experiences

Courses offered Missiology courses at master's level

Training ethos Center located in Toronto, a world class city and one of the most multi-cultural in the world.

Program introduces each of the major focii within missiology.

8 courses in core program.
23 missions/ mission related courses offered.

Profile no. 49   Canada

Established 1922
PRAIRIE BIBLE COLLEGE

Mailing address PRAIRIE BIBLE COLLEGE
Box 4000
Three Hills, AB   T0M 2N0 CANADA

Phone 403 - 443 5511   **Fax** 403 - 443 5540

Location 319 5th Avenue North, Three Hills, Alberta

Director of program Glen A. Flewelling, Co-ordinator

Teaching staff 5 Western - 3 with cross-cultural experience
0 non-Western

Languages of instruction English

Learning styles 70% formal class-room teaching
30% non-formal learning experiences

Courses offered World Mission courses in bachelor's degree
World Mission courses at certificate or diploma level

Training ethos Many opportunities on campus and in the class room to interact with a large number of international students.

Regular interaction with missionaries on campus, in the classroom and at conferences and seminars.

BA in Intercultural studies requires summer internship. BMin includes one year internship cross-culturally.

Profile no. 50   Canada

Established 1988
PRAIRIE GRADUATE SCHOOL

Mailing address   PRAIRIE GRADUATE SCHOOL
CPO Box 30096
Calgary, AB   T2H 2V8 CANADA

Phone 403 - 777 0150   **Fax**

Location   1011 Glenmore Trail S.W., Calgary

Director of program   Dr. Charlotte Bates, Dean

Teaching staff   5 Western - 2 with cross-cultural experience
0 non-Western

Languages of instruction   English

Learning styles   80% formal class-room teaching
20% non-formal learning experiences

Courses offered   Missiology degree at master's level

Training ethos   The goals of Prairie Graduate School demand a creative integration of theory, reflection and practical experience.

Besides classes and distance education courses, Prairie offers field training in cooperation with churches, missions and other ministries.

In addition to knowledge acquisition the intent is that people be global influencers and life long learners.

Profile no. 51   Canada

Established 1925

PROVIDENCE COLLEGE & SEMINARY - MAY INSTITUTE OF MISSION STUDIES

Mailing address   PROVIDENCE COLLEGE & SEMINARY
May Institute of Mission Studies
Otterburne, Manitoba R0A 1G0 CANADA

Phone 204 - 433 7488   **Fax** 204 - 433 7158

Location   as above

Director of program   Dr Jonathan J. Bonk, Director

Teaching staff   16 Western - 5 with cross-cultural experience
0 non-Western

Languages of instruction   English

Learning styles   75% formal class-room teaching
25% non-formal learning experiences

Courses offered   Missiology degree at master's level
World Mission courses in bachelor's degree
World Mission courses at certificate or diploma level
Pre-field training & orientation - 1 year internship

Training ethos   The internship year is at the heart of our program.

Students are required to spend one year in ministry in some context that will be challenging - often cross-cultural and non-traditional.

Profile no. 52   Canada

Established 1988
TRINITY WESTERN SEMINARY

Mailing address TRINITY WESTERN SEMINARY
7600 Glover Road
Langley, BC   V3A 6H4 CANADA

Phone 604 - 888 7511   **Fax** 604 - 888 5729

Location as above

Director of program Dr. Guy Saffold, Dean

Teaching staff 25 Western - 3 with cross-cultural experience
0 non-Western

Languages of instruction English

Learning styles 75% formal class-room teaching
25% non-formal learning experiences

Courses offered Missiology degree at master's level

Training ethos Trinity is located close to metro - Vancouver, one of the fastest growing multi-cultural settings in North America.

With hands-on experience in the local areas, our missions programs integrate classroom education with real life.

Profile no. 53   Canada

Established 199
WORLD MISSIONARY TRAINING CENTRE

Mailing address WORLD MISSIONARY TRAINING CENTRE
c/o Clarence Knapp, 3384 Gladwin Road
Clearbrook, BC   V2S 7C9 CANADA

Phone 604 - 859 6733   **Fax** 905 - 529 0630

Location Vancouver, British Columbia, CANADA

Director of program Ken Getty, Interim Principal

Teaching staff

Languages of instruction English

Learning styles 33% formal class-room teaching
33% non-formal learning experiences

Courses offered World Mission courses at certificate or diploma level

Training ethos A 1 year non-accredited hands-on missionary training program with practical experience amongst various ethnic groups in the lower mainland of British Columbia.

Requirements: 1 year of Bible School or equivalency. Prefer some cross cultural background or experience in missions.

Profile no. 54   Chile

Established 1984
INSTITUTO TEOLOGICO AREA METROPOLTANA

Mailing address INSTITUTO TEOLOGICO AREA METROPOLTANA
Casilla 90 - Correo 22
Santiago CHILE

Phone 56-2 634 24 66   **Fax**

Location Santiago, CHILE, South America

Director of program Juan Medina, Rector

Teaching staff 0 Western
8 non-Western - 4 with cross-cultural experience

Languages of instruction Spanish

Learning styles 100% formal class-room teaching

Courses offered World Mission courses in bachelor's degree

Training ethos Con el programa de misionologia se pretende que el estudiante graduado sirva como pastor misionero en su tierra, para posteriormente, dios mediante, salir al extranjero.

Profile no. 55 Chile

Established 1921
THEOLOGICAL INSTITUTE OF TEMUCO

Mailing address INSTITUTO TEOLOGICO DE TEMUCO
Casilla 11-D
Temuco CHILE

Phone 56-45 214212   **Fax** 56-45 215741

Location Dinamarca 578, Temuco, CHILE

Director of program Rev Charlie Woehr, Rector

Teaching staff 4 Western - 4 with cross-cultural experience
6 non-Western - 1 with cross-cultural experience

Languages of instruction Spanish

Learning styles 80% formal class-room teaching
20% non-formal learning experiences

Courses offered World Mission courses in bachelor's degree
World Mission courses at certificate or diploma level

Training ethos Our program has always been focussed on preparing leaders and pastors for the churches of various denominations.

Due to increasing mission awareness we have branched out into this area.

It is still being developed in the practical part of the training.

Profile no. 56   Colombia

Established 1976
CENTRO DE ESTUDIOS BIBLICOS "BEREA"

Mailing address CENTRO DE ESTUDIOS BIBLICOS "BEREA"
Apartado Aéreo 48160
Santa Fe de Bogotá COLOMBIA

Phone 57-1 616 4613   **Fax**

Location Calle 95 #34-37, La Castellana
Bogotá. COLOMBIA

Director of program Joy Symes de Corson

Teaching staff 2 Western - 2 with cross-cultural experience
7 non-Western - 2 with cross-cultural experience

Languages of instruction Spanish

Learning styles 80% formal class-room teaching
20% non-formal learning experiences

Courses offered World Mission courses at certificate or diploma level

Training ethos The aim of the course is to equip the student for a more effective ministry, at home or overseas, by providing the opportunity and the facilities for a concentrated study.

It is a college's concern to help the student transfer the knowledge received in the classroom to his heart, as this way it will become a part of his individual life, which in turn will produce fruit.

Profile no. 57   Colombia

Established 1944
SEMINARIO BIBLICO DE COLOMBIA

Mailing address   SEMINARIO BIBLICO DE COLOMBIA
Missiology Department
Apartado Aéreo 1141
Medellin COLOMBIA

Phone 57-4 264 2827   **Fax** 57-4 234 3132

Location   as above

Director of program   Prof. Jack Voelkel, Director

Teaching staff

Languages of instruction   Spanish

Learning styles   90% formal class-room teaching
10% non-formal learning experiences

Courses offered   Missiology degree at Licenciate level
World Mission courses in basic theology degree

Training ethos   We are a "standard" theological training institution. However we require week end practical assignments and a year of practical work as a requirement for graduation.

Of the 130 students, 19 are in the missiology department. We encourage personal contact with professors and cross-cultural experince for mission students.

Profile no. 58   Croatia

Established 1972
EVANJEOSKI TEOLOSKI FAKULTET

Mailing address   EVANJEOSKI TEOLOSKI FAKULTET
p.p. 370
54103 Osijek CROATIA

Phone 385- 54 556 466   **Fax** 385-54 556 466

Location   Cjetkova 32, Osijek, Croatia

Director of program   Dr. Peter Kuzmic

Teaching staff   12 Western - 10 with cross-cultural experience
7 non-Western - 4 with cross-cultural experience

Languages of instruction   English & Croatian

Learning styles   75% formal class-room teaching
25% non-formal learning experiences

Courses offered   World Mission courses in bachelor's degree
World Mission courses at certificate or diploma level

Training ethos   The Evanjeoski Teoloski Fakultet training program is offered in an inter-denominational, international context.

Missions training is accomplished in context of broader theological training and practical experience.

Profile no. 59 **Ecuador**

Established 1976
SEMINARIO BAUTISTA TEOLOGICO DEL ECUADOR

Mailing address   SEMINARIO BAUTISTA TEOLOGICO del ECUADOR
17-03-4724
Quito ECUADOR

Phone 593-2 551 607   **Fax**

Location   Marchena y América, Quito, ECUADOR

Director of program   David Sills, Decano

Teaching staff   6 Western - 6 with cross-cultural experience
4 non-Western - 2 with cross-cultural experience

Languages of instruction   Greek, Hebrew, Spanish, English

Learning styles   80% formal class-room teaching
20% non-formal learning experiences

Courses offered   World Mission courses in bachelor's degree
World Mission courses at certificate or diploma level

Training ethos   The SBTE Quito Center is a Baptist seminary which incorporates formal classroom instruction as well as practical work outside the classroom.

We are developing programs which will integrate seminary level education with institute TEE level work.

Our goal is involving our seminary level students in the instruction of our lower levels in order to multiply the ministry that we have in training leaders in Ecuador.

Profile no. 60   El Salvador

Established 1986
CHRISTIAN UNIVERSITY OF THE ASSEMBLIES OF GOD

Mailing address UNIVERSIDAD CRISTIANA DE LOS ASAMBLEOS DE DIOS
Facultad de Teologia/ Misiones
San Salvador EL SALVADOR

Phone 503 - 25 5046   **Fax** 503 - 25 2973

Location 27 Calle Orienta No.134
San Salvador. EL SALVADOR

Director of program D. Rance, Decano

Teaching staff 6 Western - 6 with cross-cultural experience
15 non-Western - 6 with cross-cultural experience

Languages of instruction Spanish

Learning styles 75% formal class-room teaching
25% non-formal learning experiences

Courses offered Missiology degree at master's level
World Mission courses in bachelor's degree
World Mission courses at certificate or diploma level

Training ethos The purpose of the Department of Theology of the Christian University of the Assemblies of God is to gather a faculty core of Pentecostal leaders, theologians, missiologists and educators in order to provide, develop and disciple leadership through formal and non-formal educational models to respond to the theological and missiological needs of El Salvador and the world.

Profile no. 61   Fiji Islands

Established 1983
CHRISTIAN LEADERSHIP COLLEGE

Mailing address CHRISTIAN LEADERSHIP COLLEGE
PO Box 6915
Nasinu, Suva FIJI ISLANDS

Phone 679- 340 371   **Fax** 679- 340 254

Location Daniva Road, Valelevu, Nasinu, FIJI

Director of program Jack D. Eggar, Principal

Teaching staff 10 Western - 5 with cross-cultural experience
4 non-Western - 1 with cross-cultural experience

Languages of instruction English & Fijian

Learning styles 95% formal class-room teaching
5% non-formal learning experiences

Courses offered World Mission courses in bachelor's degree
World Mission courses at certificate or diploma level
Pre-field training & orientation - 13 weeks each term

Training ethos The central focus of CLC is pastoral and missions training. With Fiji's diverse cultural and religious heritage there is a considerable opportunity to prepare leaders for ministry from around the world.

Profile no. 62   Fiji Islands

Established 1991
GLOBAL MISSION BIBLE COLEGE

Mailing address GLOBAL MISSION BIBLE COLEGE
PO Box 596
Labasa, Vanua Levu FIJI ISLANDS

Phone 679- 813 496   **Fax** 679- 813 496

Location Seniwatoa, Labasa, FIJI

Director of program Viliame Lomaloma, Principal

Teaching staff 4 Western resident but visiting teachers
2 non-Western

Languages of instruction English & Fijian

Learning styles 40% formal class-room teaching
60% non-formal learning experiences

Courses offered World Mission courses at certificate or diploma level
Pre-field training & orientation - 6 months to 1 year

Training ethos At present we are running 2 streams - one for those who had some experience in missions and another for those who had very little or no field experience but would like to be later on workers.
Full programme starting at 4 am till 10 pm, much time is given to non-formal learning experiences.

Our affiliation with New Covenant International Seminary enables our students to do graduate studies.

Our global strategy is to train foreign students (Pacific first) and to open extension centres in Solomon Islands, Vanuatu, Papua New Guinea, Kiribati etc.

Our strategy locally is to open night classes with churches and to open extension centres in the main towns, planting churches and training converts from within.

Profile no. 63　　　　　　　　　　　　　　　　　　　　France

Established 1987
BETHANIE CENTRE DE FORMATION MISSIONNAIRE

Mailing address　BETHANIE CENTRE de FORMATION MISSIONNAIRE
Le Chambon de Vorey

43800 Vorey FRANCE

Phone 33- 71 03 72 91　　**Fax** 33- 71 03 49 38

Location　127 Km south-west of Lyon, between St.Etienne and Le Puv-en-Velav

Director of program　Ross Thomas Hindman, Director

Teaching staff　2 Western - 2 with cross-cultural experience
0 non-Western

Languages of instruction　French

Learning styles　40% formal class-room teaching
60% non-formal learning experiences

Courses offered　World Mission courses at certificate or diploma level

Training ethos　Béthanie is an evangelical interdenominational training center with the goal of giving students a solid theological and practical formation enabling them to work in three general areas of ministry :
Cross-cultural missions, church planting and ministry in the local church.

Our one and two year programs consist of biblical studies, apprenticeships in ministry and a practical work program.

We also offer 5 day intensive courses once a month (October through May) for those who can't attend a full year.

Profile no. 64   Gabon

Established 1990
BETHEL BIBLE INSTITUTE

Mailing address BETHEL BIBLE INSTITUTE
B.P. 18,232
Libreville GABON

Phone 241 - 70 24 96   **Fax** 241 - 70 24 97

Location The Alliance Church of Gabon

Director of program Roland Bowman, Director

Teaching staff 5 Western - all with cross-cultural experience
2 non-Western - 0 with cross-cultural experience

Languages of instruction French

Learning styles 80% formal class-room teaching
20% non-formal learning experiences

Courses offered World Mission courses at diploma or certificate level

Training ethos We have had a pastoral and theological program for several years and are just now beginning to develop a concentration on cross-cultural mission.

We have 12 hours of courses and are looking for French texts and materials.

Profile no. 65 Germany

Established 1976
FREIE HOCHSCHULE FÜR MISSION

Mailing address FREIE HOCHSCHULE FÜR MISSION
Postfach 1129
D 70807 Korntal- Munchingen GERMANY

Phone 49- 711 83 98 71   **Fax** 49-711 83 80 545

Location Hindenburgstrasse 36,
Korntal near Stuttgart.

Director of program Dr. Helmuth Egelkraut, Dean

Teaching staff 10 Western - 7 with cross-cultural experience
0 non-Western

Languages of instruction German

Learning styles 100% formal class-room teaching

Courses offered Missiology degree at master's level

Training ethos The total instructional program is geared toward cross-cultural missionary service.

It is expected that applicants have either completed Bible college or if they are university graduates have at least 30 credit hrs. of Bible and Theology. In special cases these can be made up in residence.

About 60% of students have five years and more missionary experience. Besides there is a program of in-sevice training of not academic nature.

The special contribution of this school is studying within a community of missionaries from all over the world, spiritual formation, academic credit and degree from Columbia International University, Columbia, S.C.

Profile no. 66   Germany

Established 1978
M.V. DOULOS (OPERATION MOBILISATION)

Mailing address M.V.DOULOS (Operation Mobilisation)
Postfach 1565
74819 Mosbach GERMANY

Phone 49-6261 800 756   **Fax** 49-6261 800 746

Location The ship is continually moving from port to port !

Director of program Jimmie Christie, Training Leader

Teaching staff 8Western - 4 with cross-cultural experience
5 non-Western - 5 with cross-cultural experience

Languages of instruction English

Learning styles 20% formal class-room teaching
80% non-formal learning experiences

Courses offered

Training ethos We want to help make disciples who will make disciples among the nations.

There is a daily lecture, sermon or Bible study discussion plus week-long seminars on missiological subjects. But most of the training is "on the job" : growing in cross-cultural communication and relationships in cabin, work teams, and evangelism in each port.

Doulos training is a good foretaste & foundation for cross-cultural misssions!

Profile no. 67 Germany

Established 1988
M.V. LOGOS II (OPERATION MOBILISATION)

Mailing address M.V. LOGOS II (Operation Mobilisation)
Postfach 1565
74819 Mosbach GERMANY

Phone 49- 6261 800 756   **Fax** 49- 6261 800 746

Location On board LOGOS II

Director of program Marty Banzhaf, TrainingManager

Teaching staff Mix of Western & non-Western with cross-cultural experience

Languages of instruction English & Spanish

Learning styles 30% formal class-room teaching
70% non-formal learning experiences

Courses offered World Mission courses at certificate or diploma level
Pre-field training & orientation - 2 weeks basic ship

Training ethos Directing and facilitating the equiping and evaluative process of a mobile, multi-cultural and opportunity oriented ministry within an environment resourced for spiritual and character development with multi-input and life-direction challenges for missions.

Basic ship training takes place onshore as a pre-orientation and equipping for ship life and ministry.

Profile no. 68   Germany

Established
MISSIONSHAUS BIBELSCHULE WIEDENEST

Mailing address   MISSIONSHAUS BIBELSCHULE WIEDENEST
Postfach 1360, Olperstrasse 10
51702 Bergneustadt GERMANY

Phone 49-2261 40 92 0   **Fax** 49-22 61 40 92

Location   Wiedenest

Director of program   Klaus Brinkmann, Mission Director

Teaching staff   3 Western - 3with cross-cultural experience
0 non-Western

Languages of instruction   German

Learning styles   80% formal class-room teaching
20% non-formal learning experiences

Courses offered   World Mission courses in bachelor's degree
World Mission courses at certificate or diploma level
Pre-field training & orientation - 3 to 9 months

Training ethos   The mission training program is part of the Bible School courses which are offered as 1 year, 2 year or 3 year courses.

The latter one is meant besides others for full-time mission ministry.

Profile no. 69   Germany

Established 1899

THEOLOGISCHES SEMINAR DER LIEBENZELLER MISSION

Mailing address   THEOLOGISCHES SEMINAR der LIEBENZELLER MISSION
PO Box 1240
75375 Bad Liebenzell GERMANY

                    Phone 49-7052 17100   **Fax** 49-7052 17104

Location   Liobastrasse 17
75378 Bad Liebenzell

Director of program   Wilfried Dehn, Direktor

Teaching staff   25 Western - 4with cross-cultural experience
0 non-Western

Languages of instruction   German

Learning styles   80% formal class-room teaching
20% non-formal learning experiences

Courses offered   World Mission courses in bachelor's degree
World Mission courses at certificate or diploma level

Training ethos   Our seminary has two sections:

1. Seminary for young men.
The students receive a five-years' training in various subjects such as church planting, mission work, youth work, Sunday School work etc. These five years also include one year of practice.

2. Bible school for young women
The students receive a four years' training in the same subjects mentioned above. The course includes one year of practice.

In both cases main emphasis is laid upon training in church-planting and mission work at home and abroad.

Profile no. 70   Ghana

Established 1973
CHRISTIAN SERVICE COLLEGE

Mailing address CHRISTIAN SERVICE COLLEGE
PO Box 3110
Kumasi GHANA

Phone 233-6186   **Fax**

Location Kumasi

Director of program Mrs. Juliana Senavoe, Principal

Teaching staff 0 Western & 7 non-Western

Languages of instruction English

Learning styles 80% formal class-room teaching
20% non-formal learning experiences

Courses offered World Mission courses at certificate or diploma level

Training ethos Our aim is to train those who will become leaders of the church in these days of unrest, change, growth and theological confusion.

The programme therefore focuses on ensuring academic excellence, spitutal maturity, professional competence and missionary endurance.

Profile no. 71 Ghana

Established
GHANA CHRISTIAN COLLEGE

Mailing address GHANA CHRISTIAN COLLEGE
PO Box 5722
Accra GHANA

Phone 233-21 226 735   **Fax**

Location Abeka, Accra

Director of program Christian Adjei, Principal

Teaching staff 4 Western - 4 with cross-cultural experience
5 non-Western

Languages of instruction English

Learning styles 90% formal class-room teaching
10% non-formal learning experiences

Courses offered World Mission courses in bachelor's degree
World Mission courses at certificate or diploma level

Training ethos The diploma and certificate programs focus extensively on biblical and practical studies to prepare leaders for the church.

The B A program is designed to allow graduates to pursue post-graduate theological education.

Profile no. 72   Ghana

Established 1991
WORLD LINK UNIVERSITY

Mailing address   WORLD LINK UNIVERSITY
Box 2632
Accra GHANA

Phone 233- 21 775268   **Fax** 233- 21 775268

Location   World-wide - 10 participating centers in 10 different non-Western countries

Director of program   Dr. Seth Anyomi, Intl.Chancellor

Teaching staff

Languages of instruction   English, Asian, African, Latin American

Learning styles   50% formal class-room teaching
50% non-formal learning experiences

Courses offered   Missiology degree at doctoral level
Missiology degree at master's level
World Mission courses in bachelor's degree
World Mission courses at certificate or diploma level
Pre-field training & orientation - 1 year

Training ethos   WLU links existing missionary training centers in locations around the world, provides them with a core curriculum, a pool of inter-cultural trainers, missiologists & master teachers, expanded library resources, a data bank of academic achievements & accreditation.

Currently ten centres are affiliated with WLU. They are located in South Korea, Japan, India, Indonesia, Ghana, Nigeria, Kenya, Peru & Brazil. The international headquarters of WLU is located on the island of Batam, Indonesia.

WLU 's core curriculum allows for the specific needs of each locale, providing each student with methods of cross-cultural ministry adaptable anywhere in the world, and also presenting him with the specifics of where he is at on the globe.

Profile no. 73   Guatemala

Established 1993
CENTRAL AMERICAN CENTER FOR MISSIONARY EDUCATION (CEMCA)

Mailing address   CENTRAL AMERICAN CENTER FOR MISSIONARY EDUCATION (CEMCA)
Apdo. 129 Cod. 01901
Guatemala City GUATEMALA

                   Phone 502- 2 733 886   **Fax** 502- 2 730 532

Location   Calle Mariscal 12-15
Zona II Col. Mariscal. Guatemala

Director of program   Dr.Stanley L. Herod, Executive Director

Teaching staff   5 Western - 5 with cross-cultural experience
3 non-Western - 1 with cross-cultural experience

Languages of instruction   English / Spanish

Learning styles   50% formal class-room teaching
50% non-formal learning experiences

Courses offered   World Mission courses at certificate or diploma level
Pre-field training & orientation

Training ethos   Our program is wholly training in cross-cultural studies with a strong emphasis on supervised field training.

Three trimesters of 12 weeks - 8 weeks classroom and 4weeks field each trimester.

Profile no. 74   Guatemala

Established 1990
CENTRO DE EVANGELIZACION Y CAPACITATION MISIOLOGICA (CECAM)

Mailing address CENTRO DE EVANGELIZACION Y CAPACITATION MISIOLOGICA (CECAM)
6a. Avenida "A" 4-60 zona 1.
Guatemala ciudad. 01001 GUATEMALA

Phone 502-2 20791   **Fax** 502-2 22832

Location Iglesia Evangelica Presbiteriana Central
Primera Iglesia Evangelica de Guatemala

Director of program Lic. Fernando Mazariegos

Teaching staff 3 Western - 3 with cross-cultural experience
8 non-Western - 5 with cross-cultural experience

Languages of instruction Español

Learning styles 80% formal class-room teaching
20% non-formal learning experiences

Courses offered World Mission courses in bachelor's degree
World Mission courses at certificate or diploma level

Training ethos El Programa de CECAM está diseñado especialmente para trabajar en áreas indigenas de Guatemala.

Dentro del pénsum se encuentra el área di linguistica y sociologia de los grupos autóctonos.

Tenemos 6 graduados trabajando en áreas misioneras y un grupo de alumnos de 16. Hay un Pastor en la Iglesia que está a cargo de los Proyectos misioneros de CECAM.

Profile no. 75　　　　　　　　　　　　　　　　　　　　　Guatemala

Established 1992
CURSO DE MISIONES POR CORRESPONDENCIA

Mailing address　CURSO DE MISIONES POR CORRESPONDENCIA
Apartado Postal 555 - A
Guatemala City GUATEMALA

Phone 502-2 340964　　　**Fax** 502-2 340965

Location　　7 Avenida 7 - 07, Zona 5
Edificio El Patio. Local 116

Director of program　Lic.Fredy Gularte, Director de A.M.E.

Teaching staff

Languages of instruction　Spanish

Learning styles　nil formal class-room teaching
100% non-formal learning experiences

Courses offered　Pre-field training & orientation - 1 año

Training ethos　El curso consiste en 45 guias de estudio, distribuidas en 10 meses.

Cada mes, el estudiante es responsable de contestar las guias, investigar algunos paises, leer biografias de misioneras y devolver las tareas a la oficina.

Tambien el estudiante debe someterse a 2 examenes anuales y desarrollar un proyecto de campo.

Profile no. 76   **Guatemala**

Established 1992
FACULTAD TEOLOGICA PENTECOSTAL

Mailing address   FACULTAD TEOLOGICA PENTECOSTAL
Apdo. Postal 307
Guatemala City 01901 GUATEMALA

           Phone 502-2 91 3537   **Fax** 502-2 91 2773

Location   as above

Director of program   Ricardo E Waldrop, GENERAL

Teaching staff   2 Western - 3 with cross-cultural experience
12 non-Western - 3 with cross-cultural experience

Languages of instruction   Spanish

Learning styles   90% formal class-room teaching
10% non-formal learning experiences

Courses offered   World Mission courses in bachelor's degree

Training ethos   The program is committed to the development & teaching of Pentecostal theology which gives emphasis to wholistic mission, including the proclamation of the Gospel in word, sign & deed; discipleship formation; world evangelization;
& social transformation.

Profile no. 77   Guatemala

Established 1993
PERSPECTIVAS

Mailing address PERSPECTIVAS CONEMM
Apartado 28
01901 Guatemala City GUATEMALA

Phone 502-2 26782   **Fax**

Location   none

Director of program   David P. Rising

Teaching staff   2 Western - 2 with cross-cultural experience
15 non-Western - 10 with cross-cultural experience

Languages of instruction   Spanish

Learning styles   100% formal class-room teaching

Courses offered

Training ethos   We are using Mision Mundial, an adaptation of the U S Perspectives text book, plus adding articles produced by Latin authors. We try to use mainly Latin teachers.

Profile no. 78   Guatemala

Established 1929
SEMINARIO TEOLOGICO CENTRO AMERICANO

Mailing address SEMINARIO TEOLOGICO CENTRO AMERICANO
Apdo. 213
01901 Guatemala City GUATEMALA

Phone 502-2 710573   **Fax** 502-2 735 957

Location Av. Bolivar 30-42, Zona 3, Guatemala City

Director of program Eugenio Campos, Director Mission

Teaching staff 9 Western - 9 with cross-cultural experience
21 non-Western - 4 with cross-cultural experience

Languages of instruction Spanish

Learning styles 90% formal class-room teaching
10% non-formal learning experiences

Courses offered World Mission courses in bachelor's & masters levels
World Mission courses at certificate or diploma level

Training ethos Our centre has as its emphasis training students to understand and communicate the Scriptures. We feel this is the foundation for all effective ministry.

A very active student missions committee keeps missions before the student body, with missions emphasis week and the project of sending out students as missionaries in vacation.

Profile no. 79   Hong Kong

Established 1899
ALLIANCE BIBLE SEMINARY

Mailing address   ALLIANCE BIBLE SEMINARY
22 Peak Road
Cheung Chau HONG KONG

Phone 852- 981 0345   **Fax** 852- 981 9777

Location   as above

Director of program   Mary Chung, Lecturer

Teaching staff

Languages of instruction   Cantonese, Mandarin (English occasionally)

Learning styles   90% formal class-room teaching
10% non-formal learning experiences

Courses offered   Missiology degree at master's level
World Mission courses in bachelor's degree
World Mission courses at certificate or diploma level

Training ethos   Alliance Bible Seminary offers missiological training at master degrees level, i.e. Master of Mission and Evangelism and Master of Divinity with major in mission and evangelism, besides a program in Diploma in Mission and Evangelism.

Aside from classroom training, students are expected to do field research for their paper assignments, as well as participate in a summer mission internship, training in the mission field in cross-cultural missions (between 4- 8 weeks).

Profile no. 80   Hong Kong

Established 1987
CHINESE MISSION SEMINARY

Mailing address   CHINESE MISSION SEMINARY
P O Box 29, Shatin Central Post Office

Shatin, New Territories HONG KONG

Phone 852- 605 5515   **Fax** 852- 602 2024

Location   No.1 Kau To Village, Lai Ping Road
Shatin. N.T.

Director of program   Dr. Jonathan Chao, President

Teaching staff   0 Western
8 non-Western - 3 with cross-cultural experience

Languages of instruction   Cantonese, Mandarin

Learning styles   80% formal class-room teaching
20% non-formal learning experiences

Courses offered   World Mission courses in bachelor's degree

Training ethos   We aim at training missionaries for China emphasizing discipleship, China studies and mission.

Our programs aim at integrating academic studies with practical training and mission outreach.

One year Missionary Training Institue is held.

Profile no. 81   India

Established 1976
BEERSHEBA GOSPEL TRAINING CENTRE

Mailing address   BEERSHEBA GOSPEL TRAINING CENTRE
Waterworks Road,
Pathankot   INDIA   145 001

Phone 91-186 20005   **Fax** Nil

Location   as above

Director of program   Dr P G Vargis, President

Teaching staff   0 Western
5 non-Western - 5 with cross-cultural experience

Languages of instruction   Hindi

Learning styles   65% formal class-room teaching
35% non-formal learning experiences

Courses offered   Pre-field training & orientation courses - 2 years

Training ethos   We are training students in Language orientation; How to have cross-cultural evangelism; Homiletics. So after the completion they get a motivation to evangelise North India.

Students select a pioneer field for evangelisation and to plant churches.

Profile no. 82   India

Established 1978
CHRIST'S DISCIPLES TRAINING INSTITUTE

Mailing address   CHRIST'S DISCIPLES TRAINING INSTITUTE
Kadihati P O Ganti (N) via Ganganagar
24 Parganas, West Bengal   INDIA   743 250

Phone 91-33 551 2418   **Fax** 91-33 551 2418

Location   Calcutta (behind airport)

Director of program   Rev Dr Arabinda Dey, President

Teaching staff   0 Western
4 non-Western - 2 with cross-cultural experience

Languages of instruction   English & Bengali

Learning styles   60% formal class-room teaching
40% non-formal learning experiences

Courses offered   World Mission courses at certificate or diploma level
Pre-field training & orientation courses - 1 month

Training ethos   This programme is for pioneer missionaries who want to go to the places where the name of Christ is not known. Hardworking people are welcome.

Profile no. 83 India

Established
CHURCH GROWTH RESEARCH CENTRE, MCGAVRAN INSTITUTE

Mailing address CHURCH GROWTH RESEARCH CENTRE
McGavran Institute
Post Bag 512 Egmore
Madras   INDIA   600 008

Phone 91-44 825 5372   **Fax** 91-44 641 1803

Location 13/2 Aravamuthan Garden Street
Egmore, Madras

Director of program The Director

Teaching staff 0 Western
2 non-Western - 2 with cross-cultural experience

Languages of instruction English & vernacular as situation arises.

Learning styles nil formal class-room teaching
100% non-formal learning experiences

Courses offered Seminars and short courses

Training ethos The main objective is to enable the church planters and missionaries to develop people movement to the unreached people groups. So the target is the grass root workers and cross-cultural missionaries who are trained through church growth seminars and short courses.

Profile no. 84 India

Established 1983
CHURCH ON THE ROCK THEOLOGICAL SEMINARY

Mailing address CHURCH ON THE ROCK THEOLOGICAL SEMINARY
Dora Thota, Bhimili P.O. Box 3
Dist. Vizag, A.P.   INDIA   531 163

Phone 91-891 89514   **Fax**

Location as above

Director of program Rev Dr P.J. Titus, President

Teaching staff 0 Western
10 non-Western - 10 with cross-cultural experience

Languages of instruction English & Telugu

Learning styles 75% formal class-room teaching
25% non-formal learning experiences

Courses offered World Mission courses in bachelor's degree
World Mission courses at certificate or diploma level

Training ethos Bibliocentric-Christocentric-Charismatic-Full Gospel-Transdenominational Missiological Seminary.

M.Div., M.Min., M.Miss., M.A.(Theol). - 2 to 3 years.
B.Th. - 3 to 4 years.
G.Th. - Dip.Th., C.Th., B.K.C. - 1 to 3 years.

Profile no. 85　　　　　　　　　　　　　　　　　　　　　　　　**India**

Established 1970
FAITH THEOLOGICAL SEMINARY

Mailing address　FAITH THEOLOGICAL SEMINARY
P O Box No. 1 Manakala, Dist. Pathanamthitta
Adoor, Kerala　INDIA　691 551

Phone 91-4734 2448　　**Fax** 91-4734 2900

Location　Manakala, Adoor

Director of program　Rev K V Simon, Registrar

Teaching staff　0 Western
35 non-Western - 5 with cross-cultural experience

Languages of instruction　English & Malayalam

Learning styles　75% formal class-room teaching
25% non-formal learning experiences

Courses offered　World Mission courses in bachelor's degree
World Mission courses at certificate or diploma level
Pre-field training & orientation courses

Training ethos　"Perfecting to make perfect in Christ'"

Profile no. 86   **India**

Established 1982
FILADELFIA BIBLE COLLEGE

Mailing address FILADELFIA BIBLE COLLEGE
Rani Road, opp. Sanjay Park
Udaipur, Rajasthan INDIA 313 001

Phone 91-294 - 523346   **Fax**

Location as above

Director of program Dr Thomas Mathews

Teaching staff 0 Western
17 non-Western - all with cross-cultural experience

Languages of instruction Hindi & English

Learning styles 70% formal class-room teaching
30% non-formal learning experiences

Courses offered World Mission courses in bachelor's degree
World Mission courses at certificate or diploma level

Training ethos Training natives in evangelism & church planting.
The college aims to equip native young men and women who have recognised the call of God in their lives for pastoral leadership and evangelism, especially to reach all the unreached villages and towns of North India.

Profile no. 87   India

Established 1989
FRONTIER MISSIONS CENTRE (YWAM)

Mailing address FRONTIER MISSIONS CENTRE (YWAM)
G P O Box 127
Pune, Maharashtra   INDIA 411 001

Phone   **Fax** 91 212 659 601

Location   Schools are conducted in several cities in India and Nepal

Director of program   Steve Cochrane, SOFM Director

Teaching staff   10 Western - 10 with cross-cultural experience
10 non-Western - 10 with cross-cultural experience

Languages of instruction   English, Hindi, Nepali- by 1995 Bengali,Tamil

Learning styles   20% formal class-room teaching
80% non-formal learning experiences

Courses offered   World Mission courses at diploma or certificate level
Pre-field training & orientation courses - 12 weeks

Training ethos   YWAM is committed to knowing God and making Him known amongst the unreached peoples of the world.

Our Schools of Frontier Mission are designed to equip long-term cross-cultural missionaries in the key aspects of the task of planting indigenous self-multiplying churches amongst the unreached peoples of South Asia.

Core subjects include: Biblical mandate for missions; History of missions; Missions strategy; Cross cultural issues; Language learning; People group research; Spiritual warfare; Comparative religions.

Our training is centred around learning by doing with candidates spending 12 months field apprenticeship appplying principles learnt in the 3 months lecture phase.

In our training we value academic excellence but we

Profile no. 88 **India**

Established 1991
INDIA CENTRE FOR EVERY PEOPLE - OM INDIA

Mailing address INDIA CENTRE FOR EVERY PEOPLE (O.M. INDIA)
Logos Bhavan, Medchal Road, Jeedimetla
Secunderabad, A.P. INDIA 500 855

Phone 91- 842 863188   **Fax** 91- 842 861 457

Location as above

Director of program John Vargis, Training Director

Teaching staff 0 Western
25 non-Western - 25 with cross-cultural experience

Languages of instruction English

Learning styles 25% formal class-room teaching
75% non-formal learning experiences

Courses offered World Mission courses at certificate or diploma level

Training ethos On - the - job training.

Basic missionary training program 2 years with classroom studies and field studies.

Leadership School 2 months.

Unique to grass-roots level. Progressive to Bachelor degrees and higher.

Meeting the requirements for IMA accreditation.

Highly developmental : Discipleship, World Christians, Mission supporters, Church planting, Leadership, Ministry careering.

Profile no. 89   **India**

Established 1980

INDIAN INSTITUTE FOR CROSS- CULTURAL COMMUNICATION

Mailing address   INDIAN INSTITUTE for CROSS- CULTURAL COMMUNICATION,
Post Box 376. Andra University P.O.
Visakhapatanam, AP   INDIA   530 003

           Phone   **Fax**

Location   Nasik, Maharashtra

Director of program   Jacob C. George, Co-ordinator

Teaching staff   3 Western - 3 with cross-cultural experience
5 non-Western - 5 with cross-cultural experience

Languages of instruction   English

Learning styles   100% formal class-room teaching
No non-formal learning experiences

Courses offered   Pre-field training & orientation courses - 6 months

Training ethos   Our aim is to train nationals for Bible Translation and literacy - both cross-cultural workers as well as mother tongue speakers.

The training involves language learning principles and language analysis techniques (unwritten languages).

Profile no. 90   India

Established 1991
INDIAN INSTITUTE OF MULTI-CULTURAL STUDIES

Mailing address INDIAN INSTITUTE of MULTI-CULTURAL STUDIES
204 P L Banerjee Road, Lalgarh

Madhupur, Dist. Deoghar, Bihar   INDIA   815 353

Phone 91-6438 566   **Fax**

Location as above

Director of program Rev. S.D. Ponraj, Director

Teaching staff 0 Western
6 non-Western - 3 with cross-cultural experience

Languages of instruction English & Hindi

Learning styles 60% formal class-room teaching
40% non-formal learning experiences

Courses offered World Mission courses at certificate or diploma level
Pre-field training & orientation - 3 months

Training ethos ICMS is situated on the mission field - for regular field work.
ICMS has developed 10 mission courses with study materials.
ICMS gives balance in spirituality, academics and practicals.
ICMS is non-structured and student oriented.

Profile no. 91   **India**

Established 1987
JUBILEE MEMORIAL BIBLE COLLEGE

Mailing address   JUBILEE MEMORIAL BIBLE COLLEGE
Post Box 3465 Anna Nagar West
Madras   INDIA   600 040

                     Phone   **Fax**

Location   21 Erkkari Street, Iyyancherry
Urappakkam, Chengalpattu Dist., Tamil Nadu

Director of program   Rev P T Chandapilla

Teaching staff   0 Western
5 non-Western - 5 with cross-cultural experience

Languages of instruction   English

Learning styles   75% formal class-room teaching
25% non-formal learning experiences

Courses offered   World Mission courses in bachelor's degree

Training ethos   Training in Missions will be the central thrust of the college in all its programmes, teaching students to live according to the evangelical truths in sixty six books of the Bible.

The greater emphasis will be on the life of discipleship in godliness, faith and prayer.

Profile no. 92   **India**

Established 1989
LUTHER NEW THEOLOGICAL COLLEGE

Mailing address   LUTHER NEW THEOLOGICAL COLLEGE
Kulhan P O Challang, Sahastradhara Road
Dehra Dun, UP   INDIA   248 001

Phone 91-135 684 7256   **Fax**

Location   as above

Director of program   George Chavanikamannil, Principal

Teaching staff   0 Western
14 non-Western - 8 with cross-cultural experience

Languages of instruction   Hindi and English

Learning styles   85% formal class-room teaching
15% non-formal learning experiences

Courses offered   World Mission courses in bachelor's degree
World Mission courses at certificate or diploma level

Training ethos   Our primary goal is to equip and motivate Indian national Christians to become missionaries among people groups that are yet to be reached. Therefore we try to develop a pioneering spirit in our students.

Strong emphasis on prayer and the work of the Holy Spirit.

Profile no. 93   India

Established 1983
MISSIONARY TRAINING INSTITUTE, NAVAJEEVODAYAM CENTRE

Mailing address   MISSIONARY TRAINING INSTITUTE,
Navajeevodayam Centre
PO Box 16
Tiruvalla, Kerala   INDIA   689 101

Phone 20672 / 23507   **Fax**

Location   Navajeevodayam, Manjadi
Tiruvalla

Director of program   Dr George Samuel, Director

Teaching staff   0 Western
14 non-Western - 3 with cross-cultural experience

Languages of instruction   Malayalam & English

Learning styles   100% formal class-room teaching
non-formal learning experiences - some field visits.

Courses offered   World Mission courses at certificate or diploma level
Pre-field training & orientation courses- 1 year

Training ethos   It is a residential disciplined programme with courses conducted for 12 months. They secure a certificate if they score pass mark in the 3 terminal examinations & assignments.

The second year is also for 12 months but learning in English medium.

Profile no. 94   India

Established 1993
ORISSA SCHOOL OF EVANGELISM

Mailing address ORISSA SCHOOL OF EVANGELISM
P O Bag No. 10, B.C. Sen Road
Balasore, Orissa   INDIA   756 001

Phone 91-6782 2920   **Fax** 91-6782 65158

Location B.C.Sen Road, Balasore, Orissa

Director of program Rev. Allen Mandal, Dean

Teaching staff 0Western
3 non-Western - 3 with cross-cultural experience

Languages of instruction Oriya & English

Learning styles 95% formal class-room teaching
5% non-formal learning experiences

Courses offered World Mission courses at certificate or diploma level

Training ethos Our program is designed to expose the candidates particularly on Church planting subjects.

We also break program period for one month practical field exposure.

Profile no. 95 India

Established 1972
OUTREACH LEADERSHIP TRAINING CENTRE

Mailing address OUTREACH LEADERSHIP TRAINING CENTRE
P O Box 44
Dimapur, Nagaland INDIA 797 112

Phone 91- 3862 20480   **Fax**

Location as above

Director of program Dr Vepari Epao, Director

Teaching staff 0 Western
1 non-Western - with cross-cultural experience

Languages of instruction English

Learning styles 80% formal class-room teaching
20% non-formal learning experiences

Courses offered Pre-field training & orientation courses - 5 months

Training ethos Committed to training dedicated grass-roots Gospel workers to effectively equip and orient in cross-cultural ministry and church plantation.

Target - to train one thousand cross-cultural missionaries and mission motivators, that they may plant at least 500 churches within A D 2000.

Profile no. 96 **India**

Established 1976
OUTREACH TRAINING INSTITUTE

Mailing address OUTREACH TRAINING INSTITUTE
IEM, 7 Langford Road
Bangalore   INDIA   560 025

Phone Bagalur 4212   **Fax**

Location Arutpani Nagar, Thumanapally BPO
Berikai. Dist. Dharmapuri. Tamil Nadu

Director of program Prakash George, Director

Teaching staff 1 Western - 1 with cross-cultural experience
20 non-Western - 18 with cross-cultural experience

Languages of instruction English

Learning styles 60% formal class-room teaching
40% non-formal learning experiences

Courses offered Pre-field training & orientation courses - 20 weeks

Training ethos The emphasis of the program is to prepare potential missionaries for cross cultural missionary work.

The training provided will help people to go to a new place, settle down and start a viable ministry.

Profile no. 97 　　　　　　　　　　　　　　　　　　　India

Established 1989
SOUL WINNERS BIBLE SEMINARY (SISWA)

Mailing address　SOUL WINNERS BIBLE SEMINARY (SISWA)
Post Box 3463, Anna Nagar
Madras　　INDIA　600 040

Phone 91-44 6211967　　**Fax**

Location　as above

Director of program　V C Selwyn, Principal

Teaching staff　0 Western
9 non-Western - 4 with cross-cultural experience

Languages of instruction　English

Learning styles　75% formal class-room teaching
25% non-formal learning experiences

Courses offered　World Mission courses in bachelor's degree
World Mission courses at diploma or certificate level

Training ethos　The unique feature of our training programme is the emphasis on mission in the changing society according to the needs of people.

Practical training is compulsory.

Profile no. 98　　　　　　　　　　　　　　　　　　India

Established 1982
SOUTH ASIA INSTITUTE OF ADVANCED CHRISTIAN STUDIES (SAIACS)

Mailing address SOUTH ASIA INSTITUTE OF ADVANCED CHRISTIAN STUDIES (SAIACS)
Box 7747 Kothanur P.O.
Bangalore 560 077 INDIA

Phone 91-80 846 5235　　**Fax** 91-80 556 5547

Location SAIACS, Doddagubbi Cross Road
Kothanur PO. Bangalore

Director of program Dr Graham Houghton, Principal

Teaching staff 4 Western - 3 with cross-cultural experience
8 non-Western - 8 with cross-cultural experience

Languages of instruction English

Learning styles formal class-room teaching
non-formal learning experiences

Courses offered Missiology degree at doctoral level
Missiology degree at master's level

Training ethos Our Ethos is missiological and devotional. We cater in a pastoral way to the spiritual life and seek by all means to cultivate spiritual discipline.

Profile no. 99 India

Established 1982
UNION BIBLICAL SEMINARY - CENTRE FOR MISSION STUDIES

Mailing address UNION BIBLICAL SEMINARY
Centre for Mission Studies
Post Box 1425. Bibvewadi
Pune   INDIA 411 037

Phone 91- 212 421747   **Fax** 91- 212 423968

Location   as above

Director of program   Rev Sebastian Kim, Co-ordinator,

Teaching staff   2 Western - 2 with cross-cultural experience
8 non-Western - 8 with cross-cultural experience

Languages of instruction   English

Learning styles   80% formal class-room teaching
20% non-formal learning experiences

Courses offered   Missiology degree at master's level
World Mission courses in bachelor's degree

Training ethos   CMS is the Missiology Department of Union Biblical Seminary, Pure, India.

CMS seeks to facilitate the study of issues facing Christian missionaries in India and elsewhere by means of degree course in missiology, missiological research, seminars, consultations and publications.

Refresher course for pastors and missionaries 1 month

Summer school of communication 2 weeks

Profile no. 100   India

Established 1984
YAVATMAL COLLEGE FOR LEADERSHIP TRAINING

Mailing address   YAVATMAL COLLEGE for LEADERSHIP TRAINING,
Post Box 25
Yavatmal, Maharashtra   INDIA 445 001

Phone 91- 7232 42424   **Fax**

Location   Seminary Compound, Yavatmal, Maharashtra

Director of program   Rev. Dr. Andrew Swamidoss, Director

Teaching staff   0 Western
8 non-Western - all with cross-cultural experience

Languages of instruction   English & Hindi - separate streams

Learning styles   60% formal class-room teaching
40% non-formal learning experiences

Courses offered   World Mission courses in bachelor's degree
World Mission courses at certificate or diploma level
Pre-field training & orientation courses - 6 weeks

Training ethos   YCLT is an all-India based, grass-roots level, fully-fledged missionary training college to train cross-cultural workers.

It is managed by a registered society consisting of inter-denominational national churches and mission societies.

Learning subjects related to missions, spiritual life development and acquiring ministerial skills through field training/ministry are the three major emphases.

The concern is to equip the missionaries to reach the unreached people groups with adequate training.

Profile no. 101　　　　　　　　　　　　　　　　　　Indonesia

Established 1979
EVANGELICAL THEOLOGICAL SEMINARY OF INDONESIA

Mailing address　SEKOLAH TINGGI THEOLOGIA INJIL INDONESIA
JL. Sala Km. 11, Kotak Pos. No.4 / YKAP
Yogyakarta INDONESIA

Phone 62-274 96256　　**Fax** 62-274 96258

Location　as above

Director of program　Dr Kim Jung Yuk

Teaching staff　5 Western - 5 with cross-cultural experience
10 non-Western - 10 with cross-cultural experience

Languages of instruction　English & Indonesian

Learning styles　60% formal class-room teaching
40% non-formal learning experiences

Courses offered　Missiology degree at master's level
World Mission courses in bachelor's degree
World Mission courses at certificate or diploma level

Training ethos　Now three centres.

The plan is to have two more centres in
1　Surabaya, East Java
2　Medan, North Soematera

Profile no. 102 Indonesia

Established 1988
INSTITUT ALKITAB "RHEMA"

Mailing address INSTITUT ALKITAB "RHEMA"
Jl Hasanuddin No.6
Medan, Sumut   INDONESIA

Phone 62-61 812 360   Fax 62-61 323 563

Location as above

Director of program Dr. Benjamin Munthe, Rektor

Teaching staff 1 Western - with cross-cultural experience
17 non-Western

Languages of instruction Indonesia

Learning styles 60% formal class-room teaching
40% non-formal learning experiences

Courses offered World Mission courses in bachelor's degree
World Mission courses at certificate or diploma level

Training ethos A church-based Bible Institute with emphasis on church planting and reaching other people groups in Indonesia and abroad.

The student (present enrolment - 350 students) is involved in all aspects of local church and evangelistic ministry.

Profile no. 103 Ivory Coast

Established
ECOLE MISSIONNAIRE DU PLEIN EVANGILE EN COTE D'IVOIRE (EMPECI)

Mailing address ECOLE MISSIONNAIRE du PLEIN EVANGILE en COTE d'IVOIRE
21 B.P. 108
Abidjan 21 IVORY COAST

Phone 225- 45 22 98   **Fax** 225- 45 50 76

Location Ab idjan, (Yopougon-Toit Rouge)

Director of program Richard Borgman, Director

Teaching staff 2 Western - 2 with cross-cultural experience
3 non-Western - 1 with cross-cultural experience

Languages of instruction French

Learning styles

Courses offered World Mission courses at diploma or certificate level

Training ethos

Profile no. 104 Jamaica

Established 1986
CARIBBEAN GRADUATE SCHOOL OF THEOLOGY

Mailing address CARIBBEAN GRADUATE SCHOOL of THEOLOGY
PO Box 121 Constant Spring
Kingston 8 JAMAICA

Phone 1809- 925 7358   **Fax** 1809- 925 9129

Location 14 West Avenue, Constant Spring

Director of program Carlton Dennis

Teaching staff 6 Western - 6 with cross-cultural experience
6 non-Western - 5 with cross-cultural experience

Languages of instruction English

Learning styles 85% formal class-room teaching
15% non-formal learning experiences

Courses offered Missiology degree at master's level

Training ethos The Caribbean Graduate School of Theology has two goals for its missions programmes :

1. to train missionaries for the field;
2. to produce missionary trainers.

In fact its students will produce critically important papers for missions in the Caribbean.

Profile no. 105   Japan

Established 1949
IMMANUEL BIBLE TRAINING COLLEGE

Mailing address   IMMANUEL BIBLE TRAINING COLLEGE
1194-1 Nishihassaku-cho, Midori-ku
Yokohama 227 JAPAN

Phone 81-45 931 3533   **Fax** 81-45 931 0552

Location   as above

Director of program   Rev Dr Joshua T. Tsutada, President

Teaching staff   7 Western - 7 with cross-cultural experience
23 non-Western - 7 with cross-cultural experience

Languages of instruction   Japanese

Learning styles   50% formal class-room teaching
50% non-formal learning experiences

Courses offered   Pre-field training & orientation - 4 years

Training ethos   24 hours of residential traininG for 4 years is aimed to help students to grow into the ministers of the Gospel who can fit themselves to whatever the part of the world they are sent out.

Each one a minister whose heart and life is pure before God, practically trained, fully to be able to serve (or lead).

Profile no. 106　　　　　　　　　　　　　　　　　　　　　　Japan

Established 1975
JAPAN SUMMER INSTITUTE OF LINGUISTICS

Mailing address　JAPAN SUMMER INSTITUTE OF LINGUISTICS
4-31-7 Hamadayama, Suginami-ku
Tokyo 168 JAPAN

Phone 81-3 3313 5029　　**Fax** 81-3 3316 6002

Location　as above

Director of program　Takashi Fukuda

Teaching staff　0 Western
10 non-Western -10 with cross-cultural experience

Languages of instruction　Japanese

Learning styles　60% formal class-room teaching
40% non-formal learning experiences

Courses offered　Pre-field training & orientation - 5 weks

Training ethos　Practical training on phonetics, language learning methods, language analysis and cross-cultural communication for Japanese speaking persons.

Profile no. 107 Japan

Established 1986
MISSIONARY TRAINING CENTER

Mailing address MISSIONARY TRAINING CENTER
P O Box 1 Takaku Ots
Nasu-machi, Tochigi-ken JAPAN 325-03

Phone 81- 287 781 585   **Fax** 81-287 782 532

Location Tochigi Prefectur, Tohoku District
2 hours north of Tokyo

Director of program Rev Minoru Okuyama, Director

Teaching staff 0 Western
2 non-Western - 2 with cross-cultural experience

Languages of instruction English, Japanese & Spanish

Learning styles 90% formal class-room teaching
10% non-formal learning experiences

Courses offered World Mission courses at certificate or diploma level

Training ethos We provide bilateral training :
training Japanese going abroad; and also receiving foreign missionaries to Japan who can learn and experience different aspects of adaptation to a culture.

MTC is an international center.

Profile no. 108   Kenya

Established 1986
AFRICA INLAND CHURCH MISSIONARY COLLEGE

Mailing address AFRICA INLAND CHURCH MISSIONARY COLLEGE
P O Box 3718
Eldoret KENYA

Phone 254 321 31340   **Fax**

Location 5 Km south of Eldoret town, Kapasya area, near Limo House Surgical Clinic

Director of program Mr. Elijah Boiywo, Actg. Principal

Teaching staff 4 Western - 4 with cross-cultural experience
3 non-Western - 2 with cross-cultural experience

Languages of instruction English (primary), Kiswahili (secondary)

Learning styles 70% formal class-room teaching
30% non-formal learning experiences

Courses offered World Mission courses at certificate or diploma level

Training ethos A I C Missionary College offers a 15 Month cross-cultural missionary training program.

Husbands and wives are trained together to be team-mates
in ministry.

Practical field experience is a vital part of training - a 2 week observation and research practical and later a supervised,
4 month missionary field experience.

We train students from many African nations, and denominations.

Profile no. 109   Kenya

Established 1990

NAIROBI EVANGELICAL GRADUATE SCHOOL OF THEOLOGY

Mailing address   NAIROBI EVANGELICAL GRADUATE SCHOOL of THEOLOGY
PO Box 24 686 - Karen
Nairobi KENYA

Phone 254-2 720 837   **Fax** 254-2 720 253

Location   as above

Director of program   Dr. Stanley Mutunga

Teaching staff   1 Western - 1 with cross-cultural experience
1 non-Western - 1 with cross-cultural experience

Languages of instruction   English

Learning styles   90% formal class-room teaching
10% non-formal learning experiences

Courses offered   Missiology degree at master's level

Training ethos   Ours is a 2 year programme designed for preparation for Christian practical work either within one's culture or in cross-cultural settings.

We cater for students from Africa as well as Western countries.

Profile no. 110   Kenya

Established 1980
NAIROBI INTERNATIONAL SCHOOL OF THEOLOGY

Mailing address   NAIROBI INTERNATIONAL SCHOOL OF THEOLOGY
P O Box 60954
Nairobi KENYA

Phone 254-2 720 837   **Fax** 254-2 720 253

Location   Mtito Andei Road, Kilimani Estate, Nairobi

Director of program   Dr. Lazarus Servyange, Principal

Teaching staff   8 Western - 8 with cross-cultural experience
6 non-Western - 3 with cross-cultural experience

Languages of instruction   English

Learning styles   75% formal class-room teaching
25% non-formal learning experiences

Courses offered   World Mission courses in bachelor's degree

Training ethos   The purpose if NIST is to build and train Christ-like servant leaders who are equipped to help fulfill the Great Commission in Africa and the world.

We offer three post-graduate degrees in the multi-cultural, multi-denominational urban context of Nairobi, Kenya.

We are fully accredited by ACTEA.

We offer in-depth study of the Scriptures, integrated with the practical application of God's truth in ministry.

Profile no. 111   Kenya

Established 1992
SCHOOL OF MISSIONS, EASTERN REGION (AEA)

Mailing address   SCHOOL OF MISSIONS, Eastern Region
Association of Evangelicals of Africa (AEA)
P O Box 49332
Nairobi KENYA

Phone 254-2 720 220   **Fax** 254-2 710 254

Location   A.E.A. Staff compound, Riara Rd, Nairobi

Director of program   Lucy Muguiyi, Training

Teaching staff   6 Western - 6 with cross-cultural experience
9 non-Western - 8 with cross-cultural experience

Languages of instruction   English

Learning styles   60% formal class-room teaching
40% non-formal learning experiences

Courses offered   Pre-field training & orientation - 10 months

Training ethos   We emphasise a lot on Christ-like character and life impartation.

Trainers and trainees live together and trainers model out the life of Christ.

Students go for four months practical field work among the unreached people of Kenya in between their 6 months academic training,

Profile no. 112　　　　　　　　　　　　　　　　　　　　　Korea

Established 1974
ASIAN CENTER FOR THEOLOGICAL STUDIES & MISSION (ACTS)

Mailing address　ASIAN CENTER for Theological Studies & Mission
(ACTS)
187 Choongieong-Ro 3ga. Sudaemoon-Gu
Seoul　120-751 KOREA

Phone 82-2 363 3247　　**Fax** 82-2 393 3789

Location　as above

Director of program　Dr Han, Chul Ha, President

Teaching staff　9 Western - 9 with cross-cultural experience
20 non-Western - 3 with cross-cultural experience

Languages of instruction　English

Learning styles　70% formal class-room teaching
30% non-formal learning experiences

Courses offered　Missiology degree at doctoral level
Missiology degree at master's level
World Mission courses at certificate or diploma level

Training ethos　Our program was born 20 years ago under the idea of Asian church leaders that Asia must be evangelized through Asians and that Asian church leaders must be trained in Asia.

All the overseas Asian students are under full scholarship. including room and board.

Profile no. 113   Korea

Established 1987

CROSS-CULTURAL MISSIONARY TRAINING INSTITUTE

Mailing address   CROSS-CULTURAL MISSIONARY TRAINING INSTITUTE
395-153 Suhkyo-dong, Mapo-ku
Seoul   121-210 KOREA

Phone 82-2 335 0592   **Fax** 82-2 335 4951

Location   as above

Director of program   Rev Jong Yoon Lee, Director

Teaching staff   0 Western
3 non-Western - 2 with cross-cultural experience

Languages of instruction   Korean (mostly) & English

Learning styles   60 % formal class-room teaching
40%   non-formal learning experiences

Courses offered   Pre-field training & orientation - 6 months

Training ethos   Purpose :
A. To train missionary candidates in cross-cultural mission and language.
B. To study and research various mission information and seek co-operation of Korean churches and other mission organizations for world mission.

Contents of the Training :
A. Theoretical basis for cross-cultural mission
B. Language training in English
C. Cross-cultural witnessing practice within the country and in short-term missions abroad; seminars and Retreats

Partnership relations with certain foreign mission organizations eg AIM, IEM, People International, World Concern etc.

Profile no. 114   Korea

Established 1968
EAST WEST CENTER FOR MISSIONS, RESEARCH AND DEVELOPMENT

Mailing address EAST WEST CENTER for MISSIONS, RESEARCH AND DEVELOPMENT
110-1 Wolmoon. Paltan. Hwasung.
Kunggi-do   445-910 KOREA

Phone 82-339 353 1301   **Fax** 82-339 52 5234

Location as above

Director of program   Dr David J Cho, General Director

Teaching staff   7 Western - 7 with cross-cultural experience
7 non-Western - 5 with cross-cultural experience

Languages of instruction

Learning styles   70% formal class-room teaching
30% non-formal learning experiences

Courses offered   Missiology degree at masters & doctoral levels
World Mission courses in bachelor's degree
World Mission courses at certificate or diploma level
Pre-field training & orientation - 6 months

Training ethos   1. Missionary internship which leads to M.A. in Missiology

2 Doctor of Missiology program

3. Publication of Asian Missions Advance - missiological periodical

4. Publication of Missiological books and periodicals

Profile no. 115   Korea

Established
FULL GOSPEL WORLD MISSIONARY TRAINING CENTER

Mailing address   FULL GOSPEL WORLD MISSIONARY TRAINING CENTER, Yoido Full Gospel Church
P O Box 7
Seoul KOREA

                      Phone 82-2 780 7296   **Fax** 82-2 780 0180

Location   Education Center 9th Floor of Yoido Full Gospel Church
11 Yoido dong. Seoul

Director of program   Tai-Heung Yang

Teaching staff   1 Western
4 non-Western

Languages of instruction   Korean

Learning styles   70% formal class-room teaching
30% non-formal learning experiences

Courses offered   Pre-field training & orientation - 10 months

Training ethos   Aspirant requirement:
Graduate from 4 year Bible school or Seminary.

                     Daily 2 hour prayer meeting and 1 hour bible reading and 2 months' overseas training are mandatory in this course.

Profile no. 116   Korea

Established 1987
GLOBAL MISSIONARY TRAINING CENTER

Mailing address GLOBAL MISSIONARY TRAINING CENTER
231-188 Mok 2 Dong, Yang Chun Ku
Seoul   158-052 KOREA

Phone 82-2 649 3197   **Fax** 82-2 647 7675

Location as above

Director of program Dr David Taiwoong LEE

Teaching staff 0 Western but visiting teachers
5 non-Western - 2 with cross-cultural experience

Languages of instruction Korean

Learning styles 40% formal class-room teaching
60% non-formal learning experiences

Courses offered Pre-field training & orientation - 9 months

Training ethos Since Korean mission needs both pioneers and leaders, we are emphasising a balanced missionary training (education). We offer not only an overview of missiological subjects (at Master's degree level) but also practical side of discipleship training.

Profile no. 117   Korea

Established 1991
GLOBAL PROFESSIONALS TRAINING INSTITUTE

Mailing address GLOBAL PROFESSIONALS TRAINING INSTITUTE
Kang Nam P O Box 1052
Seoul 135-610 KOREA

Phone 82-2 537 2043   **Fax** 82-2 595 7809

Location as above

Director of program Don Ho Soon, General Secretary

Teaching staff 0 Western
5 non-Western - 3 with cross-cultural experience

Languages of instruction Korean

Learning styles 50% formal class-room teaching
50% non-formal learning experiences

Courses offered Pre-field training & orientation - 1 year

Training ethos GPTI runs the training program with following objectives so that the tent maker missionary candidates are sufficiently prepared :

Orient with creative access areas and tent making ministry in those areas.

Cultivate the ability to survive in a no-outside-help situation; crisis management etc

Learn to carry out cross cultural evangelization and discipling

Understand the mission and learn how to approach other religions

Learn to adapt cross culturally - language acquisition, cross-cultural communication etc.

Profile no. 118   **Korea**

Established 1992
INSTITUTE OF ISLAMIC STUDIES

Mailing address   INSTITUTE of ISLAMIC STUDIES
CPO Box 9024
Seoul   100 - 690 KOREA

Phone 82-2 532 7574   **Fax** 82-2 535 0465

Location   as above

Director of program   Dr. Chun Chae Ok, Chairperson

Teaching staff   0 Western
5 non-Western - 5 with cross-cultural experience

Languages of instruction   Korean

Learning styles   100% formal class-room teaching

Courses offered   Pre-field training & orientation - 10 weeks course
(only on Saturdays)

Training ethos   Activities :

1. Research & Publications of Islamic study materials in Korean language.

2. Education & Orientation - invite recognized scholars in Islam to lead short seminar courses. Regular ten seminar courses held once a week.

3. Dialogue & Co-operation - serve as a liaison among Far East countries in the study of Islam.

Aim is to create reconciliatory attitudes rather than be trapped in the long-lasting tensions between Muslims & Christians.

Profile no. 119   Korea

Established
INTERNATIONAL MISSIONARY TRAINING INSTITUTE

Mailing address INTERNATIONAL MISSIONARY TRAINING
INSTITUTE
PO Box 93. Sudaimoon
Seoul   120-600 KOREA

Phone 82-2 702 1513   **Fax** 82-2 706 2546

Location   as above

Director of program   Rev Heavystone Choi

Teaching staff   0 Western
7 non-Western - 3 with cross-cultural experience

Languages of instruction   English & Korean

Learning styles

Courses offered   World Mission courses at certificate or diploma level

Training ethos

Profile no. 120   Korea

Established 1989
KEHC MISSION HOME

Mailing address KEHC MISSION HOME
890-56 Daechi-dong, Kangnam-ku
Seoul   138 160 KOREA

Phone 82-2 501 7072   **Fax** 82-2 501 7074

Location Karak Bon-dong 13-17
Songpa-ku, Soul

Director of program Rev Im Chul Jae, President

Teaching staff 3 Western - 3 with cross-cultural experience
3 non-Western - 3 with cross-cultural experience

Languages of instruction

Learning styles 50% formal class-room teaching
50% non-formal learning experiences

Courses offered World Mission courses at certificate or diploma level
Pre-field training & orientation

Training ethos 1. KEHC is a denominational missionary training

2. 4 fold Gospel (regeneration, sanctification, divine healing & second coming of the Lord) centered education

3. Evangelism, church planting, training of the nationals, partnership mission.

Profile no. 121 — Korea

Established 1975
KOREAN CENTER FOR WORLD MISSIONS

Mailing address   KOREAN CENTER for WORLD MISSIONS
55 Yang Jai-dong, Sucho-ku
Seoul   137-130 KOREA

Phone 82-2 570 7003   **Fax** 82-2 574 2374

Location   as above

Director of program   Dr Sang-Bok Kim, Executive Director

Teaching staff   0 Western
20 non-Western - 5 with cross-cultural experience

Languages of instruction   Korean

Learning styles   100% formal class-room teaching
0% non-formal learning experiences

Courses offered   World Mission courses at certificate or diploma level
Pre-field training & orientation

Training ethos   We offer course by course Certificate of completion and Diploma for a year program.

Training pastors and lay people mostly in Korean language

Profile no. 122   Korea

Established 1994
KOREAN WORLD MISSIONS TRAINING INSTITUTE

Mailing address   KOREAN WORLD MISSIONS TRAINING INSTITUTE
P O Box 94 Choong Jongno
Seoul 120-650 KOREA

Phone 82-2 363 7091   **Fax** 82-2 393 8462

Location   Hope Prayer Retreat Center, Kwnag Joo, Kyunggido

Director of program   Dr Bong Rin Ro, Director

Teaching staff   1 Western - with cross-cultural experience
11 non-Western - 8 with cross-cultural experience

Languages of instruction   Korean - English used in some lectures

Learning styles   90% formal class-room teaching
10% non-formal learning experiences

Courses offered   Missiology degree at master's level

Training ethos   This is a new program to train missionary candidates in cooperation with 15 minor mission agencies including 5 denominational missions.

It is a joint venture sponsored by the Korean World Missions Association (KWMA).

Two four week sessions in the spring and autumn each will be conducted for some 60 candidates and the students have to stay at the center.

The courses are connected with the Asian Center for Theological Studies and Mission (ACTS) which will give credit for the courses.

Profile no. 123   Korea

Established 1988
KOSIN MISSIONARY TRAINING INSTITUTE

Mailing address   KOSIN MISSIONARY TRAINING INSTITUTE (KMTI)
243 - 17 Jungli-Dong, Daedug-Gu
Daejeon City 306-050 KOREA

                         Phone   **Fax**

Location   as above

Director of program   Rev Sam Chan Kwak, President

Teaching staff   2 Western - 2 with cross-cultural experience
5 non-Western - 5 with cross-cultural experience

Languages of instruction   English & Korean

Learning styles   90% formal class-room teaching
10% non-formal learning experiences

Courses offered   Pre-field training & orientation - 3 weeks twice an year -

Training ethos   Program :

       1   Early morning: morning devotion time (am 5.30 - 6.30) with sermon.

       2   Morning: General lectures about missions.

       3   Afternoon: English study (2 or 3 hours)

       4   Evening: field study and prayer meeting.

Profile no. 124   Korea

Established 1982
MISSIONARY TRAINING INSTITUTE ,
PRESBYTERIAN CHURCH OF KOREA

Mailing address MISSIONARY TRAINING INSTITUTE
Presbyterian Church of Korea
58 - 10 Banpo-dong, Seocho-ku
Seoul   137-040 KOREA

Phone 82-2 593 8487, 8   **Fax** 82-2 535 9953

Location   as above

Director of program   Dr Young-jun Son, Director

Teaching staff   11 Western - 7 with cross-cultural experience
0 non-Western

Languages of instruction   English

Learning styles   80% formal class-room teaching
20% non-formal learning experiences

Courses offered   World Mission courses at certificate or diploma level

Training ethos   MTI training consists of three pillars:
Biblical and theological training; practical linguistic training and the acquisition of practical skills.

Each candidate is a member in an anglophone environment where ten native speakers of English interact with over one hundred Korean missionary candidates in a residential setting, during a month long training and fifty for three months.

Studying Missiolgy in this environment means better equipping for future work overseas where international interaction is a requirement for witness and team work and partnership relationships.

Theology and Biblical studies are conducted without translation in English language so that our graduates can teach in Bible colleges overseas whare English is the

Profile no. 125　　　　　　　　　　　　　　　　　　　　Korea

Established 1990
OM MISSIONARY TRAINING CENTRE

Mailing address　OM MISSIONARY TRAINING CENTRE
　　　　　　　　　PO Box 120 Kang Nam
　　　　　　　　　Seoul　　KOREA

　　　　　　　　Phone 82-2 568 1436　　　**Fax** 82-2 561 1869

Location　　　as above

Director of program　Johnny J.H. Song, Director

Teaching staff　2 Western - 2 with cross-cultural experience
　　　　　　　　2 non-Western - 2 with cross-cultural experience

Languages of instruction　Korean & English

Learning styles　60% formal class-room teaching
　　　　　　　　40% non-formal learning experiences

Courses offered　Pre-field training & orientation - 4 months

Training ethos　Our training is to provide a practical learning experience for those who are planing to go overseas for cross-cultural work.

　　　　　　　　We emphasise creative methods of learning, ability to adjust into inter cultural minstry and study on mission, anthropology, theology, cross-cultural communication.

Profile no. 126   Korea

Established 1994
WORLD MISSION TRAINING CENTER, KOREA BAPTIST THEOLOGICAL SEMINARY

Mailing address   WORLD MISSION TRAINING CENTER,
Korea Baptist Theological Seminary
San 14. Haki-Dong. Yusung
Taejon 305-358 KOREA

                      Phone 82-42 825 1330   **Fax** 82-42 825 1354

Location   as above

Director of program   Dr Hyun Mo Lee, Director

Teaching staff

Languages of instruction   Korean

Learning styles   100% formal class-room teaching

Courses offered   Missiology degree at master's level
World Mission courses in bachelor's degree
World Mission courses at certificate or diploma level

Training ethos   The missionary training program will start from 1996.

Profile no. 127　　　　　　　　　　　　　　　　　　Mexico,

Established 1981
INSTITUTO BETANIA, A.C.

Mailing address　INSTITUTO BETANIA, A.C.
　　　　　　　　　Apdo. Postal 27
　　　　　　　　　C.P. 78700 Matehuala, S.L.P. MEXICO

　　　　　　　　　Phone 52-488 20582　　**Fax** 52-488 27688

Location　　　　Matehala, San Luis Potosi, Northern Mexico

Director of program　Kerry A. Olson, Director

Teaching staff　5 Western - 5 with cross-cultural experience
　　　　　　　　　4 non-Western - 4 with cross-cultural experience

Languages of instruction　Spanish

Learning styles　60% formal class-room teaching
　　　　　　　　　40% non-formal learning experiences

Courses offered　World Mission courses in bachelor's degree
　　　　　　　　　World Mission courses at certificate or diploma level

Training ethos　Training and equipping Mexicans to complete the Great Commission of Christ with particular emphasis in training cross-cultural workers for the indigenous peoples of Mexico and the 10/40 window.

Profile no. 128   Mexico

Established 1986
WORLD MISSIONS INSTITUTE OF MEXICO

Mailing address   WORLD MISSIONS INSTITUTE of MEXICO
Apartado .798
Morelia, Mich.oacan   58000 MEXICO

Phone 52-43 24 2531   **Fax** 52-43 241881

Location   Libramento Ote. No. 220
Moreliua. Michoacan

Director of program   Robin Steen, Director

Teaching staff   2 Western - 1 with cross-cultural experience
1 non-Western - 0 with cross-cultural experience

Languages of instruction   Spanish

Learning styles   50% formal class-room teaching
50% non-formal learning experiences

Courses offered   World Mission courses in bachelor's degree
World Mission courses at certificate or diploma level

Training ethos   Our vision is to train Mexican nationals for cross-cultural missionary service within and without of Mexico.

Our doctrine is conservative and our training includes large amounts of time in practical service in Mexican and indigenous ministry.

Profile no. 129   Netherlands

Established 1967
CENTRALE PINKSTER BIJBELSCHOOL

Mailing address   CENTRALE PINKSTER BIJBELSCHOOL
Barneveldse weg 11
6741 LH Lunteren NETHERLANDS

Phone 31-83 882 312   **Fax** 31-83 884 4609

Location   as above

Director of program   Dr. C. Laan, Director

Teaching staff   10 Western - 9 with cross-cultural experience
0 non-Western

Languages of instruction   Dutch

Learning styles   76% formal class-room teaching
24% non-formal learning experiences

Courses offered   World Mission courses in bachelor's degree

Training ethos   We are a four year Institute of Higher Education recognised by the Dutch government for the training of teachers of religion and ministers/missionaries. (BA equivalent).

Dutch language only. Pentecostal.

Government scholarships for Dutch and Flemish students

Profile no. 130   Netherlands

Established 1973
EVANGELISCHE BIJBEL SCHOOL

Mailing address EVANGELISCHE BIJBEL SCHOOL
Postbus 171
3940 AD Doorn NETHERLANDS

Phone 31-3430 15096   **Fax**

Location Postweg 18, Doorn

Director of program A. Stringer

Teaching staff 16 Western - 4 with cross-cultural experience
0 non-Western

Languages of instruction Dutch

Learning styles 70% formal class-room teaching
30% non-formal learning experiences

Courses offered World Mission courses in bachelor's degree
World Mission courses at certificate or diploma level
Pre-field training & orientation - 10 months intership

Training ethos The EBS is an accredted Higher Institute of Vocational Training, offering 1 propedentic year, 2 years of intensive theoretical education and a 4th year of intern- ship.

Lectures are in Dutch. Reading material mainly in English. Working know;ledge of Dutch is indispensable!

Profile no. 131   Netherlands

Established 1994
IN DE RUIMTE BIJBELSCHOOL

Mailing address IN DE RUIMTE BIJBELSCHOOL
Postbus 16

3760 AA Soest NETHERLANDS

Phone 31-2155 24433   **Fax**

Location as above

Director of program H. H. ter Welle, Director

Teaching staff 8 Western - 1 with cross-cultural experience
0 non-Western

Languages of instruction Dutch

Learning styles 80% formal class-room teaching
20% non-formal learning experiences

Courses offered World Mission courses in bachelor's degree

Training ethos Our learning ethos is based on 2 Tim 2:2.

We desperately want to integrate theological education and experience in our program.

The missionary experience is generally not cross-cultural. However, students may engage in a longer working ezperience abroad.

Profile no. 132   Netherlands

Established 1990
SCHOOL OF FRONTIER MISSIONS "HEIDEBEEK" (YWAM)

Mailing address   SCHOOL of FRONTIER MISSIONS "Heidebeek" (YWAM)
Mussen kampse weg 32
8181 PK Heerde NETHERLANDS

Phone 31-5782 1534   **Fax** 31- 5782 4276

Location   as above

Director of program   Stephen Anderson

Teaching staff   90% Western - most with cross-cultural experience
10% non-Western - all with cross-cultural experience

Languages of instruction   English

Learning styles   50% formal class-room teaching
50% non-formal learning experiences

Courses offered   Pre-field training & orientation - 3 month lecture phase plus 2 year commitment to the field

Training ethos   The School of Frontier Missions (SOFM) is targeting unreached peoples (cross-culturally).

On the field you will be placed in a team.

A pre-requisite to the SOFM is a 6 months' discipleship training school (DTS) including a 3 months field trip.

DTS & SOFM are both held at Heidebeek. School at Heidebeek has highly qualified teachers and a good communication network to all corners of the earth.

Profile no. 133   Netherlands

Established 1989
THE EURO MISSIONARY TRAINING COLLEGE

Mailing address The EURO MISSIONARY TRAINING COLLEGE
Hagelkruisstraat 19

5835 BD Beugen NETHERLANDS

Phone 31-8856 1314   **Fax** 31-8856 2777

Location as above

Director of program Rev Lindsay J McKenzie, Principal

Teaching staff 6 Western - 6 with cross-cultural experience
0 non-Western

Languages of instruction English

Learning styles 70% formal class-room teaching
30% non-formal learning experiences

Courses offered World Mission courses at certificate or diploma level

Training ethos The aim of the Euro MTC is to provide students with training for cross-cultural ministry.

In the light of Matt.24:14 and 28:19/20, the command to the church is to make disciples and the methodology is to go, to teach and to baptise.

Therefore the college exists to prepare students for effective fulfillment of the commission to make disciples of all peoples.

Profile no. 134　　　　　　　　　　　　　　　　　　　　Netherlands

Established 1985
TYNDALE THEOLOGICAL SEMINARY

Mailing address　TYNDALE THEOLOGICAL SEMINARY
Egelantier straat 1
1171 JM Badhoevedorp NETHERLANDS

Phone 31-20 659 6455　　**Fax** 31-20 659 8303

Location　as above

Director of program　Dr Arthur P. Johnston, President

Teaching staff　4 Western - 4 with cross-cultural experience
0 non-Western

Languages of instruction　English

Learning styles　90% formal class-room teaching
10% non-formal learning experiences

Courses offered　Missiology degree at master's level

Training ethos　Bible Institute/Christian College graduates can study for a one year masters in missiology.

Those with 3-4 years of post-high school secular studies can enrol for a 2 year Masters in Missiology or a three year ganeral ministry degree (M.Div) with missions emphasis.

Courses taught in intensive blocks allowing a wide range of visiting professors.

Profile no. 135   New Zealand

Established 1922
BIBLE COLLEGE OF NEW ZEALAND

Mailing address   BIBLE COLLEGE of NEW ZEALAND
Department of Mission Studies
Private Bag
Henderson, Auckland 8 NEW ZEALAND

                 Phone 64- 9 837 0675   **Fax** 64- 9 837 4209

Location   221 Lincoln Road, Henderson
Auckland 8

Director of program   Dr John Roxborogh, Head of Dept.

Teaching staff   20 Western - 13 with cross-cultural experience
0 non-Western

Languages of instruction   English

Learning styles   80% formal class-room teaching
20% non-formal learning experiences

Courses offered   Missiology degree at masters or doctoral level
    - supervised by Australian College of Theology
World Mission courses in bachelor's degree
World Mission courses at certificate or diploma level
Pre-field training & orientation

Training ethos   Our aim is to help all our students have confidence about wherever it is God is calling them to be & what ever it is God is calling them to do.

We cater for a diversity of students with different ministry and mission tracks.

We seek not only to inspire and challenge but also to inform candidly & realistically, facing mission issues of our time from a strong Biblical, theological and historical base.

Profile no. 136   New Zealand

Established 1989
CENTRE FOR MISSION DIRECTION

Mailing address CENTRE for MISSION DIRECTION
P O Box 31-146
Ilam, Christchurch 8030 NEW ZEALAND

Phone 64-3 342 7711   **Fax** 64-3 342 8410

Location 70 Nortons Road, Avonhead, Christchurch

Director of program Dr. Bob Hall, National Co-ordinator

Teaching staff not applicable

Languages of instruction English

Learning styles 100% formal class-room teaching

Courses offered World Mission courses at certificate or diploma level

Training ethos Basic programme focus is the Perspectives on the World Christian Movement course. Taught through out NZ in various locations.

Profile no. 137　　　　　　　　　　　　　　　　New Zealand

Established 1969
FAITH BIBLE COLLEGE

Mailing address　FAITH BIBLE COLLEGE
　　　　　　　　　　Private Bag
　　　　　　　　　　Tauranga NEW ZEALAND

　　　　　　　　　　Phone 64- 7 544 2463　　**Fax** 64- 7 544 1923

Location　　　　　Welcome Bay Road, Tauranga

Director of program　Rev Des Short, Principal

Teaching staff　　20 Western - 14 with cross-cultural experience
　　　　　　　　　　1 non-Western - with cross-cultural experience

Languages of instruction　English

Learning styles　67% formal class-room teaching
　　　　　　　　　　33% non-formal learning experiences

Courses offered　World Mission courses at diploma or certificate level

Training ethos　Courses at Faith have a strong missions emphasis.

　　　　　　　　　　There are two courses each year commencing February & July. Each course runs for 40 weeks, including a 12 weeks' field assignment.

Profile no. 138 New Zealand

Established 1975
GLO BIBLE & MISSIONARY COLLEGE

Mailing address GLO BIBLE & MISSIONARY COLLEGE
P O Box 390, Te Awamutu NEW ZEALAND

Phone 64-7 871 - 4582 **Fax** 64-7 871 - 4425

Location Cambridge Road, Te Awamutu

Director of program Kevin White, Missions Director

Teaching staff 4 Western - 3 with cross-cultural experience
0 non-Western

Languages of instruction English

Learning styles 40% formal class-room teaching
60% non-formal learning experiences

Courses offered World Mission courses at certificate or diploma level
Pre-field training & orientation - 20 weeks

Training ethos The missionary training programme is a post-graduate course designed to develop cross-cultural ministry skills.

Participants are required to submit evidence of having completed biblical studies to diploma level.

The programme has a high degree of self-directed project work under expert mentors to develop field skills.

The programme is designed on a modular basis and can be planned to suit individual needs.

Profile no. 139   New Zealand

Established 1986
NEW COVENANT INTERNATIONAL BIBLE COLLEGE

Mailing address   NEW COVENANT INTERNATIONAL BIBLE COLLEGE
P O Box 13-470
Onehunga, Auckland 6 NEW ZEALAND

Phone 64-9 634 1709   **Fax** 64-9 634 4046

Location   75 The Mall, Onehunga, Auckland

Director of program   Bryan Johnson

Teaching staff   4 Western - 2 with cross-cultural experience
1 non-Western with cross-cultural experience

Languages of instruction   English

Learning styles   70% formal class-room teaching
30% non-formal learning experiences

Courses offered   Missiology degree at doctoral level
World Mission courses in bachelor's degree
World Mission courses at certificate or diploma level

Training ethos   A NZ - based mission-oriented training programme, especially suited to non-primary English speakers, offering meaningful cross-cultural communication, ministry and evangelism experiences with a multi- national student body from Asia, Africa and the Pacific.

Global view Christianity, language acquisition and urban ministry and church planting modules available in a 1 year to 3 years' course depending on candidates prior learning and future mission plans.

NZ Qualifications Authority - approved courses.

Profile no. 140　　　　　　　　　　　　　　　　　　New Zealand

Established 1958
NEW ZEALAND ASSEMBLY BIBLE SCHOOL

Mailing address　N.Z. ASSEMBLY BIBLE SCHOOL
20 Palmer Avenue
Kelston, Auckland NEW ZEALAND

Phone 64-9 818 5112　　**Fax** 64-9 818 4518

Location　as above

Director of program　Rev C. Doug Hewlett, Principal

Teaching staff　6 Western - 3 with cross-cultural experience
0 non-Western

Languages of instruction　English

Learning styles　80% formal class-room teaching
20% non-formal learning experiences

Courses offered　World Mission courses at certificate or diploma level
Pre-field training & orientation - 2 years

Training ethos　A number of missionary candidates take pre-field Biblical and theological training with us.

Missiological courses are offered within the full-time Diploma in Old Testament and New Testament Studies (1 yr.) and the Advanced Diploma in Theology and Christian Ministry (2 year).

In the first year a 15 lecture course is given on world missions. Attendance at a weekend missionary camp/seminar is compulsory. In addition, an elective of 6 hours plus 6 hours of personal preparation introduces students to further aspects of world missions.

A second year missiology paper is offered. Also students may select a missiological topic to research for the Advanced Diploma. The diploma courses are approved by the NZ Qualifications Authority.

Profile no. 141   Nigeria

Established 1992
AGAPE SCHOOL OF MISSIONS

Mailing address   AGAPE SCHOOL of MISSIONS
P O Box 80
Barkin Ladi, Plateau State NIGERIA

Phone 234-73 53110   **Fax** 234-73 53110

Location   Green Pastures, Kassa
Barkin Ladi Local Government Area. Plateau State

Director of program   Naomi Famonure

Teaching staff   0 Western
12 non-Western - 12 with cross-cultural experience

Languages of instruction   English

Learning styles   60% formal class-room teaching
40% non-formal learning experiences

Courses offered   Pre-field training & orientation - 10 months

Training ethos   Much emphasis is placed on discipleship and missions training, which aim at character building and having the trainees' visions transformed into actions as cross-cultural communicators.

There is much interaction between trainers and trainees.

Trainees are exposed to a 3 months" field/faith trip.

Profile no. 142   Nigeria

Established 1975
CALVARY MINISTRIES, SCHOOL OF MISSIONS

Mailing address CALVARY MINISTRIES, SCHOOL of MISSIONS,
PO Box 6001
Jos, Plateau State NIGERIA

Phone 234-73-57892   **Fax** 234-73-57892

Location

Director of program Joshua Kadon, Training Secretary

Teaching staff   0 Western
10 non-Western - each with cross-cultural experience

Languages of instruction English

Learning styles 50% formal class-room teaching
50% non-formal learning experiences

Courses offered Pre-field training & orientation - 1 year

Training ethos Emphasis on Christian living and cross-cultural missiology/Biblical training.

Profile no. 143　　　　　　　　　　　　　　　　　　　　Nigeria

Established 1993
CHRISTAC SCHOOL OF MISSIONS & DEVELOPMENT

Mailing address　CHRISTAC SCHOOL of MISSIONS & DEVELOPMENT
　　　　　　　　　P O Box 1293
　　　　　　　　　Sagamu, Ogun State NIGERIA

　　　　　　　　　Phone　　　　　　**Fax**

Location　　　　Oke Ate Village, Sagamu, Ogun State

Director of program　David Odukoya, Director

Teaching staff　　0 Western
　　　　　　　　　4 non-Western - 2 with cross-cultural experience

Languages of instruction　English

Learning styles　40% formal class-room teaching
　　　　　　　　　60% non-formal learning experiences

Courses offered　Pre-field training & orientation - 12 months

Training ethos　Modular course system, learner-centred.

　　　　　　　　　Emphasis on wholistic approach and innovations to missions.

　　　　　　　　　Courses include community organising, primary health care, introductory French (optional).

Profile no. 144 Nigeria

Established
CHRISTIAN LEADERSHIP & MISSIONARY TRAINING INSTITUTE

Mailing address CHRISTIAN LEADERSHIP & MISSIONARY TRAINING INSTITUTE
GPO Box 10335
Ibadan, Oyo State NIGERIA

Phone 234-22 415478   **Fax**

Location as above

Director of program 'Tunde Oloyede, Director

Teaching staff 1 Western- with cross-cultural experience
4 non-Western- 2 with cross-cultural experience

Languages of instruction English

Learning styles

Courses offered Courses on World Mission at diploma level - one year

Training ethos

Profile no. 145　　　　　　　　　　　　　　　　　　　Nigeria

Established 1981
CHRISTIAN LEADERSHIP & MISSIONS INSTITUTE

Mailing address　CHRISTIAN LEADERSHIP & MISSIONS INSTITUTE
　　　　　　　　　　PO Box 2449
　　　　　　　　　　Warri NIGERIA

　　　　　　　Phone 234-53 234010　　**Fax**

Location　　1 Edobor Street, Okurode- Urhobo, Warri

Director of program　Rev. Dr. Nathan Madeyi, Principal

Teaching staff　0 Western
　　　　　　　　　7 non-Western - 4 with cross-cultural experience

Languages of instruction　English

Learning styles　90% formal class-room teaching
　　　　　　　　　　10% non-formal learning experiences

Courses offered　World Mission courses at diploma or certificate level

Training ethos　Intensive class-room work.

　　　　　　　　　Students are assigned to work with pastors in different church locations for a specific period. Students and the resident pastor report on a daily basis.

　　　　　　　　　The School supervises/ visits the student while on the field.

Profile no. 146 Nigeria

Established 1989
CHRISTIAN MISSIONARY FOUNDATION (CMF) SCHOOL OF MISSIONS

Mailing address CHRISTIAN MISSIONARY FOUNDATION,
School of Missions
U. I. P O Box 9890
Ibadan NIGERIA

Phone 234-22 314 955   **Fax**

Location Idere, Ifeloju Lga, Ogyo State

Director of program Edet G. Offong, Principal

Teaching staff 4 Western - 4 with cross-cultural experience
19 non-Western - 5 with cross-cultural experience

Languages of instruction English

Learning styles 60% formal class-room teaching
40% non-formal learning experiences

Courses offered Pre-field training & orientation - 12 months

Training ethos Our program focuses on acquisition of knowledge of God, His word and the world to whom He sends us.

Development of the Christian character as well as skills needed by missionaries on the fields.

Our priorities are to train labourers for unreached people groups through partnering with churches, mission agencies and groups.

Profile no. 147   Nigeria

Established 1994
GOFAMINT SCHOOL OF WORLD MISSIONS

Mailing address GOFAMINT - Gospel Faith Mission Int., - Missions Department, U..I. P O Box 20956 Ibadan, Oyo State NIGERIA

Phone 234-22 415 015   **Fax**

Location Tinuoye Estate

Director of program Evangelist Z.I. Ilori, Principal

Teaching staff 1 Western with cross-cultural experience
10 non-Western - 6 with cross-cultural experience

Languages of instruction English

Learning styles 60% formal class-room teaching
40% non-formal learning experiences

Courses offered World Mission courses at certificate or diploma level

Training ethos The students are feeding together, cook for themselves and do other duties together. Discipline is highly enforced to a high degree. Student who could not perform up to expectation may be given rural church planting certificate.

Profile no. 148   Nigeria

Established 1989
LIFE TRAINING CENTRE

Mailing address LIFE TRAINING CENTRE
PO Box 3
Dekina, Kogi State NIGERIA

Phone   **Fax**

Location Odu - Ofugo Village, Dekina District, Kogi State

Director of program Dr John E Apeh, President

Teaching staff 0 Western
4 non-Western - all with cross-cultural experience

Languages of instruction English

Learning styles 75% formal class-room teaching
25% non-formal learning experiences

Courses offered World Mission courses at diploma or certificate level
Pre-field training & orientation

Training ethos Life Training Centre is a missionary training institute which offers courses in missions, cross-cultural studies as well as Bible & Theology.

We also offer vocational courses such as welding, animal husbandry, piggery, rabbitry, appropriate technology, printing, sheet metal works.

Our goal is to prepare self-sustaining indigenous missionaries who could go out to reach unreached people groups without depending solely on external support.

Profile no. 149　　　　　　　　　　　　　　　　　　Nigeria

Established 1988
NIGERIA CENTRE FOR WORLD MISSION

Mailing address　NIGERIA CENTRE FOR WORLD MISSION
G P O Box 221, Dugbe
Ibadan, Oyo State NIGERIA

Phone 234-22 312 413　　**Fax**

Location　Behind Government College, Oluwatedo Street
Apata Ganga, Ibadan

Director of program　Prophet M.O. Salawu, President

Teaching staff　4 Western - 3 with cross-cultural experience
7 non-Western - 5 with cross-cultural experience

Languages of instruction　English

Learning styles　60% formal class-room teaching
40% non-formal learning experiences

Courses offered　World Mission courses at certificate or diploma level

Training ethos　The students go on two practical field trips before the expiration of their studies.

After five months of rigorous classroom training, they will go on field trip.

They live a prayer life by doing night vigil every day.

Profile no. 150   Nigeria

Established 1985
NIGERIA EVANGELICAL MISSIONARY INSTITUTE (NEMI)

Mailing address NIGERIA EVANGELICAL MISSIONARY
INSTITUTE (NEMI)
PO Box 5878
Jos, Plateau State NIGERIA

Phone   **Fax**

Location as above

Director of program Rev O.A. Adekoya, Principal

Teaching staff 3 Western - 3 with cross-cultural experience
8 non-Western - 8 with cross-cultural experience

Languages of instruction English

Learning styles 50% formal class-room teaching
50% non-formal learning experiences

Courses offered Pre-field training & orientation - 15 months

Training ethos It is a practical cross-cultural train ing programme with high quality academic work and field orientation.

Field work takes half of the training time.

Profile no. 151   Nigeria

Established 1975
SCHOOL OF DISCIPLESHIP AND MISSIONS (SCODAM)

Mailing address SCHOOL of DISCIPLESHIP and MISSIONS (SCODAM)
GPO Box 1550
Ibadan, Oyo State NIGERIA

Phone 234-22 313352   **Fax**

Location Plot 11-13 Abedeji Okubadejo Lay-out
Scout Camp Challenge, Ibadan

Director of program Rev. Nicholas D. Osameyam

Teaching staff 0 Western
5 non-Western - 3 with cross-cultural experience

Languages of instruction English

Learning styles 60% formal class-room teaching
40% non-formal learning experiences

Courses offered Pre-field training & orientation - 9 months

Training ethos Students are trained and sent to the field.

Students arrange for personal accommodation for now. A permanent site has been acquired but is yet to be developed.

Profile no. 152　　　　　　　　　　　　　　　　　　　　　Nigeria

Established 1993
SCHOOL OF MISSIONARY STUDIES

Mailing address　SCHOOL OF MISSIONARY STUDIES
　　　　　　　　　UIPO Box 19488
　　　　　　　　　Ibadan, Oyo State NIGERIA

　　　　　　　　　Phone 234-22 413 845　　**Fax**

Location　　Olode Village via Ibadan

Director of program　Evangelist Samson Agboaye, Missions Director

Teaching staff　0 Western
　　　　　　　　10 non-Western - 10 with cross-cultural experience

Languages of instruction　English

Learning styles　50% formal class-room teaching
　　　　　　　　　50% non-formal learning experiences

Courses offered　World Mission courses at certificate or diploma level
　　　　　　　　　Pre-field training & orientation - 1 to 2 weeks

Training ethos　The thrust of our training in relation to cross-cultural missions is relating missions to practical missionary needs.

Focus is made on areas like drama, medical missions, creative writing, etc as well as courses like discipleship, cross-cultural missions, research methods, tent-making, prayer/spiritual warfare, practicals. etc.

Profile no. 153 Nigeria

Established 1991
THE REDEEMED CHRISTIAN SCHOOL OF MISSIONS

Mailing address THE REDEEMED CHRISTIAN SCHOOL of MISSIONS
P O Box 220
Ede, Osun State NIGERIA

Phone   **Fax**

Location Ede Town, Osun State

Director of program Yinka John Adeyemi, Principal

Teaching staff 0 Western
5 non-Western - 2 with cross-cultural experience

Languages of instruction English

Learning styles 60% formal class-room teaching
40% non-formal learning experiences

Courses offered World Mission courses at certificate or diploma level

Training ethos The school approach to training is centered on the TOTAL MAN

1 A missionary needs to be strengthened and grounded in his/her own spiritual life

2 A missionary needs to develop some understanding and skills concerning the cross-cultural nature of his/her task

3 A missionary needs some practical skills that will help him to live in an unfamiliar enviorenment.

Profile no. 154   Nigeria

Established 1959
UNITED MISSIONARY THEOLOGICAL COLLEGE

Mailing address   UNITED MISSIONARY THEOLOGICAL COLLEGE
P O Box 171
Ilorin, Kwara State NIGERIA

Phone 234- 221 703   **Fax**

Location   Murtala Mohammed Way, Ilorin

Director of program   Rev. Dr. M.F. Akangbe, Provost

Teaching staff

Languages of instruction   English

Learning styles   95% formal class-room teaching
5%   non-formal learning experiences

Courses offered   World Mission courses in bachelor's degree
World Mission courses at certificate or diploma level

Training ethos   UMTC is mainly geared toward training pastors and Bible knowledge teachers.

However there is a very active missions club doing cross-cultural outreach and a growing student interest in missions will we hope result in more missions courses in future. We offer only 2 or 3 courses now.

Profile no. 155 Nigeria

Established
WORLD OUTREACH BIBLE INSTITUTE

Mailing address   WORLD OUTREACH BIBLE INSTITUTE
P O Box 462
Sulejah, Niger State NIGERIA

Phone 234-9 500 552   **Fax**

Location   as above

Director of program   Rev P.O. Omeja, Principal

Teaching staff

Languages of instruction   English

Learning styles

Courses offered   World Mission courses in bachelor's degree
World Mission courses at diploma or certificate level

Training ethos   We organize a 2 year diploma and 2 year B.Th. degree programme that includes courses on missions.

Admissions : 2 intakes yearly - January & September

Profile no. 156   Norway

Established 1898
FJELLHAUG MISSION SEMINARY

Mailing address FJELLHAUG MISSION SEMINARY
Sinsenveien 15
N- 0572 Oslo NORWAY

Phone 47- 22 37 90   **Fax** 47- 22 37 8014

Location as above

Director of program Dagfinn Solheim, Academic Dean

Teaching staff 11 Western - 7 with cross-cultural experience
0 non-Western

Languages of instruction Norwegian & English

Learning styles 75% formal class-room teaching
25% non-formal learning experiences (1 year internship)

Courses offered Missiology degree at master's level

Training ethos Our four year program leads up to the M.Div. equivalent.

More than 90% of our students go abroad as missionaries.

We try to keep a good balance between spiritual growth, practical skills and academic standards.

Our emphasis lies on a sound Biblical basis with cross-cultural knowledge.

Profile no. 157   Norway

Established 1984
GÅ UT SENTERET,
NORWEGIAN SANTAL MISSION

Mailing address GÅ UT SENTERET, Norwegian Santal Mission

2090 Hurdal NORWAY

Phone 47- 63 98 77 77   **Fax** 47- 63 98 70 71

Location 70 Km.north of Oslo

Director of program Ingvard Hageberg, Principal

Teaching staff 6 Western - 3 with cross-cultural experience
0 non-Western

Languages of instruction Norwegian

Learning styles 80% formal class-room teaching
20% non-formal learning experiences

Courses offered Pre-field training & orientation - 10 months

Training ethos

Profile no. 158   Norway

Established 1843
THE SCHOOL OF MISSION & THEOLOGY

Mailing address The SCHOOL of MISSION & THEOLOGY
Misjonsveien 34
4024 Stavanger NORWAY

Phone 47- 51 62 10   **Fax** 47-51 62 25

Location as above

Director of program Tor Jorgensen

Teaching staff 17 Western - 8 with cross-cultural experience
1 non-Western with cross-cultural experience

Languages of instruction Norwegian & English

Learning styles 75% formal class-room teaching
25% non-formal learning experiences

Courses offered Missiology degree at doctoral level
Missiology degree at master's level
World Mission courses in bachelor's degree
World Mission courses at certificate or diploma level
Pre-field training & orientation - 1 year

Training ethos The faculty is fully recognised by the government.

It was founded to educate pastors and lay-people to become missionaries and its history goes back to 1843, owned by
the Norwegian Missionary Society.

Today (1994) 150 students.

Profile no. 159   Papua New Guinea

Established 1970
BETHEL BIBLE COLLEGE

Mailing address BETHEL BIBLE COLLEGE
P O Box 6166
Boroko NEW GUINEA

Phone 675 254 103   **Fax** 675 256 578

Location Suburb of Tokarara, Port Moresby

Director of program Pastor Barry Silverback

Teaching staff

Languages of instruction English & Pidgin

Learning styles 25% formal class-room teaching
75% non-formal learning experiences

Courses offered Pre-field training & orientation

Training ethos Affiliated with Christian Revival Crusade (Pentecostal)

2 or 3 years Bible college,
Institute on evangelism 9 months

Courses are designed to equip national/international students for ministry, locally/cross-culturally.

A strong emphasis on character development, practical ministry and Bible knowledge.

Our graduates are serving in PNG, Fiji, Philippines, India, Pakistan, Australia & NZ.

Profile no. 160   Papua New Guinea

Established 1964
CHRISTIAN LEADERS' TRAINING COLLEGE

Mailing address   CHRISTIAN LEADERS' TRAINING COLLEGE
PO Box 382
Mt Hagen, WHP NEW GUINEA

Phone 675 562 311   **Fax** 675 522 797

Location   10 Km. west of Banz in the Western Highlands

Director of program   Dr Bruce Renich, Principal

Teaching staff   7 Western - 4 with cross-cultural experience
5 non-Western - 0 with cross-cultural experience

Languages of instruction   English

Learning styles   80% formal class-room teaching
20% non-formal learning experiences

Courses offered   World Mission courses at certificate or diploma level
Pre-field training & orientation - 6 months

Training ethos   Our missions program includes subjects integrated into the Diploma of Theology program, ; an occasional 6 month Introduction to Missions course ; and an annual 7-day emphasis on missions in our "Launch out" program.

We are in the process of developing a missiology course at Bachelor degree level.

The TEE program has also prepared a new Missions course.

Profile no. 161   Papua New Guinea

Established 1977
CHRISTIAN TRAINING CENTRE

Mailing address CHRISTIAN TRAINING CENTRE
Free Mail Bag Service
Boroko NEW GUINEA

Phone   **Fax**

Location Mapodo, Western Province

Director of program Wakeya Bowaliya, Principal

Teaching staff 1 Western with cross-cultural experience
3 non-Western - 3 with cross-cultural experience

Languages of instruction English & Gogodala (vernacular)

Learning styles 50% formal class-room teaching
50% non-formal learning experiences

Courses offered Pre-field training & orientation - 3 years

Training ethos We give training to tribal groups who have had no training leaders so that they can go back and help their own churches and establish branch churches.

We also give extra training to those who had their training elsewhere to further their Biblical knowledge - those who are already out in the field or in various Bible Schools.

Profile no. 162   **Paraguay**

Established 1990
CENTRO DE EVANGELISMO Y MISIONES BETANIA

Mailing address CENTRO de EVANGELISMO y MISIONES BETANIA
Casilla de Correo 3045
Asunción PARAGUAY

Phone 595- 21 234395   **Fax** 595-21 292240

Location Camino Luque - Yukyry - Costa Garay 7 Compania Luque

Director of program Pastor Benides A. Bergamo

Teaching staff 8 Western - with cross-cultural experience
0 non-Western

Languages of instruction Spanish

Learning styles 50% formal class-room teaching
50% non-formal learning experiences

Courses offered Pre-field training & orientation

Training ethos Our prospectus has the information about our course. It's a basic course. We don't offer a cross-cultural training.

Profile no. 163   Peru

Established 1977
ESCUELA MISIOLOGICA LATINO AMERICANA

Mailing address ESCUELA MISIOLOGICA LATINO AMERICANA
Apartado 1488
Lima 100 PERU

Phone 51-14 284 557   **Fax** 51-14 454 929

Location   Magdalena - Daniel Alcides Carrión No 351

Director of program   Obed R. Alvarez

Teaching staff   0 Western
                       24 non-Western

Languages of instruction   Ingles, Español, Quechua/Aymara

Learning styles   50% formal class-room teaching
                       50% non-formal learning experiences

Courses offered   World Mission courses in bachelor's degree
                       World Mission courses at certificate or diploma level

Training ethos   Incluimos prospecto.

Profile no. 164   **Peru**

Established 1988
INSTITUTO MISIOLOGICO AMAZONICO

Mailing address   INSTITUTO MISIOLOGICO AMAZONICO
Apartado 1710
Lima 100 PERU

                       Phone   **Fax**

Location   In several places in Peru, mostly Lima and Pucallpa

Director of program   Peter Hocking, Director

Teaching staff   0 Western
10 non-Western - 10 with cross-cultural experience

Languages of instruction   Spanish

Learning styles   50% formal class-room teaching
50% non-formal learning experiences

Courses offered   World Mission courses at certificate or diploma level
Pre-field training & orientation - 1 month

Training ethos   This is a cross-cultural missionary training program, seeking to provide a proper balance between theory, character formation and field experience linked with discipleship.

The training is non-denominational.

Field experience is given in Andean and jungle tribal cultures.

Profile no. 165 Philippines

Established 1982
ALLIANCE BIBLICAL SEMINARY

Mailing address ALLIANCE BIBLICAL SEMINARY
CPO Box 1095
1099 Manila PHILIPPINES

Phone 63-2 98 47 07 **Fax**

Location 101 Dangay Street, Veterans Vi;lage, Project 7
Ouezon Citv

Director of program Dr David Strong, Assoc. Professor of

Teaching staff 6 Western - 6 with cross-cultural experience
6 non-Western - 2 with cross-cultural experience

Languages of instruction English

Learning styles 85% formal class-room teaching
15% non-formal learning experiences

Courses offered Missiology degree at master's level
World Mission courses at certificate or diploma level

Training ethos Alliance Biblical Seminary is recognized by the Philippines Department of Education, Culture and Sports and is accredited by the Asia Theological Association and the Association of Theological Schools in Southeast Asia.

Graduate-level programs of one, two and three years are offered.

Profile no. 166   Philippines

Established 1964
ASIA PACIFIC THEOLOGICAL SEMINARY (AOG)

Mailing address ASIA PACIFIC THEOLOGICAL SEMINARY (AOG)
P O Box 377
Baguio City, 2600 PHILIPPINES

Phone 63-74 442 6977   **Fax** 63- 74 442 6378

Location 444 Ambuklao Road, Baguio City

Director of program The Librarian

Teaching staff 7 Western - 7 with cross-cultural experience
5 non-Western - 5 with cross-cultural experience

Languages of instruction English

Learning styles 90% formal class-room teaching
10% non-formal learning experiences

Courses offered Missiology degree at master's level
World Mission courses at diploma or certificate level

Training ethos APTS offers the opportunity for students to take a variety of missions courses as part of a Master of Arts degree in ministry or Master of Divinity degree.

A 15 unit graduate Certificate in Missions is also available.

Profile no. 167 Philippines

Established 1974
ASIAN SEMINARY OF CHRISTIAN MINISTRIES

Mailing address ASIAN SEMINARY OF CHRISTIAN MINISTRIES
P O Box 133 MCPO, Makati
1299 Metro Manila PHILIPPINES

Phone 63-2 819 0697 **Fax** 6-32 819 5127

Location ACCM Building, 102 Valero Stereet, Salcedo Village Makati

Director of program Dr Miguel Alvarez, President

Teaching staff 6 Western - 6 with cross-cultural experience
12 non-Western - 4 with cross-cultural experience

Languages of instruction English

Learning styles 60% formal class-room teaching
40% non-formal learning experiences

Courses offered Missiology degree at master's level
World Mission courses in bachelor's degree
World Mission courses at certificate or diploma level
Pre-field training & orientation - 3 months

Training ethos ASCM offers a learning process in real-life situations.

It focuses on the Asian perspective of the ministry in Asia. It aims towards China Missions, Muslim Ministries, the Buddhist world and the Hindu Challenge.

Missionaries can take a 2 or 3 year training program or a 1 to 3 months module that enables the student to go deep into the mission field.

Profile no. 168　　　　　　　　　　　　　　　　　　　　　Philippines

Established 1969
ASIAN THEOLOGICAL SEMINARY

Mailing address　ASIAN THEOLOGICAL SEMINARY
Cross-cultural Studies program
O. C. C P O Box 1454
Quezon City 1154 PHILIPPINES

Phone 63-2 923 0667　　**Fax** 63-2 923 0669

Location　54 Scout Madriñan, Quezon City

Director of program　Dr Larry W. Caldwell, Director

Teaching staff　9 Western - 9 with cross-cultural experience
15 non-Western - 4 with cross-cultural experience

Languages of instruction　English

Learning styles　80% formal class-room teaching
20% non-formal learning experiences

Courses offered　Missiology degree at master's level
World Mission courses at certificate or diploma level

Training ethos　Asian Theological Seminary offers mission training for missionaries and missionary candidates who desire course credit at the graduate level from an academic institution recognized world wide.

There are two options for study:

1 At the 3 year M Div level with a missions major.

2 At the 1 year certificate of cross-cultural studies level.

Most missions courses require extensive out of class field work. Mission exposure trips are offered twice each year.

Profile no. 169   Philippines

Established 1970
DISCIPLESHIP TRAINING SCHOOL (YWAM)

Mailing address   DISCIPLESHIP TRAINING SCHOOL (YWAM)
P O Box 1195 Ortigas Center
1651 Pasig, Metro Manila PHILIPPINES

Phone 63-2 631 1681   **Fax** 63-2 631 7660

Location   Antipolo Rizal, Baguio City (English/Koreans)
Davao City (English/German)

Director of program   Eli Dayo, Training Director

Teaching staff   4Western - 3 with cross-cultural experience
3 non-Western - 3 with cross-cultural experience

Languages of instruction   English, English-Korean , English-German

Learning styles   60% formal class-room teaching
20% non-formal learning experiences

Courses offered   Pre-field training & orientation - 6 months

Training ethos   A DTS is designed to prepare the Christian messenger for the task of world evangelism.

It has strong emphasis on character development and personal application of truth.

Content of course includes:
A) The character and ways of God ; how to hear His voice

B) Personal character development ; principles for healthy relationships

C) The Christian's relationship in the Word
D The Christian's relationship to the lost
E) The Christian's stand against the enemy.

Profile no. 170　　　　　　　　　　　　　　　　　　　Philippines

Established 1994
GREAT COMMISSION MISSIONARY TRAINING CENTER

Mailing address GREAT COMMISSION MISSIONARY TRAINING CENTER
PO Box 12838. Ortigas Center Post Office
1605 Pasig, MetroManila PHILIPPINES

Phone 63-2 922 2105　　　**Fax** 63-2 921 0212

Location 28 Circumferential Road, Antipolo, Rizal

Director of program Dr Met Castillo, President

Teaching staff 2 Western - 2 with cross-cultural experience
4 non-Western - 4 with cross-cultural experience

Languages of instruction English

Learning styles 70% formal class-room teaching
30% non-formal learning experiences

Courses offered World Mission courses at diploma or certificate level

Training ethos GCMTC trains Asian missionary candidates for cross-cultural ministry.

Training is on three levels : formal(class-room and seminars); non-formal or practicum; and informal (through community experience and inter-action with staff and missionaries).

It focuses on practical, pre-field training - 12 weeks in class-room followed by 4 weeks field practicum.

Profile no. 171　　　　　　　　　　　　　　　　　Philippines

Established 1989
INTERNATIONAL TRAINING INSTITUTE FOR MISSIONS

Mailing address　INTERNATIONAL TRAINING INSTITUTE for MISSIONS
ACPO Box 128
Quezon City PHILIPPINES

Phone 63-2 996622　　　**Fax**

Location

Director of program　Rev Yong-Joong Cho, Director

Teaching staff　0 Western
4 non-Western - 2 with cross-cultural experience

Languages of instruction　English - Korean in some cases

Learning styles　30% formal class-room teaching
70% non-formal learning experiences

Courses offered　Pre-field training & orientation - 4 to 5 months

Training ethos　Missionary training arm of Partners for World Mission, Philippines

Profile no. 172 Philippines

Established 1966
LOMMASSON ALLIANCE BIBLE INSTITUTE

Mailing address LOMMASSON ALLIANCE BIBLE INSTITUTE
Lapuyan
Zamboanga del Sur 7037 PHILIPPINES

Phone   **Fax**

Location as above

Director of program Rev Manuel Labadia, Director

Teaching staff 0 Western
7 non-Western - 1 with cross-cultural experience

Languages of instruction English, Cebuano & Subanen dialect

Learning styles 75% formal class-room teaching
25% non-formal learning experiences

Courses offered World Mission courses at certificate or diploma level

Training ethos Basically the students are given three solid years of learnings facts and principles related to the ministry.

In their fourth year they are assigned for a year in the field to get a feel of what it is like to be a minister. After a year they return to the school for their senior year.

However while in school they are allowed to experience contact in the community for the discovery of spiritual gifts, set their preference to which tribal group will they work as local missionaries.

Profile no. 173 Philippines

Established 1961
PHILIPPINE MISSIONARY INSTITUTE

Mailing address PHILIPPINE MISSIONARY INSTITUTE
Biga, Silang
Cavite 2702 PHILIPPINES

Phone 63- 832 9391   **Fax** 63- 96 435 0042

Location

Director of program Rev Arsenio P Dominguez, Principal

Teaching staff

Languages of instruction English

Learning styles 60% formal class-room teaching
40% non-formal learning experiences

Courses offered

Training ethos Training pioneer missionaries for rural unreached areas.

Profile no. 174　　　　　　　　　　　　　　　　Philippines

Established 1990
PHILIPPINE RESOURCES OF CHRISTIAN LITERATURE & INFORMATION MINISTRIES (PROCLAIM)

Mailing address　PROCLAIM - Philippine Resources of Christian Literature & Information Ministries
15 Gueguesangen. Sta. Barbara
Pangasinan 2419 PHILIPPINES

　　　　　　　　　Phone　　　　　　　　Fax

Location　Sapang, Sta. Barbara, Pangasinan

Director of program　Pastor Rolando E Santiago

Teaching staff　0 Western
4 non-Western - 3 with cross-cultural experience

Languages of instruction　English & Tagalog

Learning styles　25% formal class-room teaching
75% non-formal learning experiences

Courses offered　Pre-field training & orientation - 1 to 2 years

Training ethos　The PROCLAIM Training Centre is designed to disciple students towards a life time of practical missions involvement.

It operates on a module basis, with five phases in a span of one year; character development training; evangelism strategies; theological foundations; spiritual warfare praying & missions exposure.

Profile no. 175   Singapore

Established 1983
ASIA EVANGELISTIC FELLOWSHIP
SCHOOL OF MISSIONS & EVANGELISM

Mailing address ASIA EVANGELISTIC FELLOWSHIP
School of Missions & Evangelism

Balestier Estate P O Box 485 SINGAPORE 9132

Phone 65- 538 8355   **Fax** 65- 533 5117

Location Courses held in conjunction with Singapore Bible College Overseas in Lalitpur,Nepal & Yangon, Myanmar

Director of program Jonathan James, Director

Teaching staff 1 Western with cross-cultural experience
6 non-Western - all with cross-cultural experience

Languages of instruction English , Burmese , Hindi, Nepali

Learning styles 50% formal class-room teaching
50% non-formal learning experiences

Courses offered World Mission courses at certificate or diploma level
Pre-field training & orientation - 6 months

Training ethos Contextualised training to mobilise nationals to serve in missions and church planting within their own cultures.

1 Practical - hands-on experience in ministry and outreach

2 Goal focused - training geared towards church planting

3 Discipleship oriented - not more than 10 per intake in a live-in situation

Profile no. 176   Singapore

Established 1985
ASIAN CROSS CULTURAL TRAINING INSTITUTE

Mailing address   ASIAN CROSS CULTURAL TRAINING INSTITUTE
Raffles City P O Box 1052 SINGAPORE 9117

Phone 65 - 339 8598   **Fax** 65 - 334 0405

Location   161 Jalan Loyang Besar, Singapore

Director of program   Melville Szto, Dean

Teaching staff   1 Western with cross-cultural experience
4 non-Western - 4 with cross-cultural experience

Languages of instruction   English

Learning styles   40% formal class-room teaching
60% non-formal learning experiences

Courses offered   Pre-field training & orientation - 4 months

Training ethos   ACTI is a post-seminary and pre-field course for missionaries and tentmakers.

It's a Singapore based training institute helping Asian and Western churches and mission agencies to prepare their candidates for cross-cultural ministry.

ACTI offers up-to-date mission knowledge and strategy, helps trainees chart their course ahead and strengthens their spiritual life in cross-cultural contexts. Lectures are given by experienced missionaries on cross-cultural life and ministry, missiological and practical issues, study and research.

Trainees have opportunities to experience cross-cultural community living, to involve in a Singapore church and to visit mission organizations. It is a course sponsored and approved by several internationlized mission

Profile no. 177   Singapore

Established 1988
BETHANY SCHOOL OF MISSIONS

Mailing address BETHANY SCHOOL of MISSIONS
Raffles City PO Box 143 SINGAPORE 9117

Phone 65 339 5722   **Fax** 65 339 0337

Location as above

Director of program D. Michael Crow, Director of Training

Teaching staff 2 Western - 2 with cross-cultural experience
2 non-Western - 2 with cross-cultural experience

Languages of instruction English & hopefully Mandarin by 1995

Learning styles 70% formal class-room teaching
30% non-formal learning experiences

Courses offered Missiology degree at master's level
World Mission courses in bachelor's degree
World Mission courses at certificate or diploma level
Pre-field training & orientation - 2 weeks

Training ethos The purpose of Bethany is to provide "Strategic Missionary Training for the Greater 10/40 window".

Bethany is "Third wave" in theology and utilizes formal, informal and non-formal methodologies for -

Training trainers of misssionaries - to plant training programs in 10/40 window countries;

Training cross-cultural missionaries - to plant churches among unreached peoples;

Training non-traditional missionaries - to plant disciples in restricted access nations.

Up to 30 adjunct faculty.

11 modules with 5 courses of 2 weeks per module.

Profile no. 178   Singapore

Established 1968
DISCIPLESHIP TRAINING CENTRE

Mailing address DISCIPLESHIP TRAINING CENTRE
33A Chancery Lane SINGAPORE 1130

Phone 65 256 3208   **Fax** 65 256 2705

Location as above

Director of program Rev Dr Bryan Hardman, Dean

Teaching staff 1 Western with cross-cultural experience
3 non-Western - 3 with cross-cultural experience

Languages of instruction English

Learning styles 80% formal class-room teaching
20% non-formal learning experiences

Courses offered World Mission courses at certificate or diploma level

Training ethos We are a small community (20 students & 4 teachers) which includes singles, marrieds & families from approx. 10 different Asian & 3 different Caucasian backgrounds.

We believe that this intercultural living fleshes out the classroom instruction and helps prepare students to share as they relate to cultures other than their own.

Profile no. 179   **Singapore**

Established 1994
SINGAPORE BIBLE COLLEGE

Mailing address SINGAPORE BIBLE COLLEGE
Diploma in Intercultural Ministry
Farrer Road P O Box 257 SINGAPORE 9128

Phone 65 466 4677   **Fax** 65 466 4980

Location 9-15 Adam Road, Singapore

Director of program Dr. Ola Tulluan, Dean

Teaching staff 8 Western - 6 with cross-cultural experience
7 non-Western - 4 with cross-cultural experience

Languages of instruction English

Learning styles 75% formal class-room teaching
25% non-formal learning experiences

Courses offered Missiology degree at master's level

Training ethos The Diploma in Intercultural Ministry is designed for university graduates or holders of other tertiary degrees who are preparing for cross-cultural missionary service.

The program is both practical and foundational.

It is offered with an option of full-time (one year) or part-time study.

Profile no. 180   Singapore

Established 1979
THEOLOGICAL CENTRE FOR ASIA

Mailing address THEOLOGICAL CENTRE for ASIA

Farrer Road P O Box 90 SINGAPORE 9128

Phone 65 460 1207   **Fax** 65 467 6005

Location 21-23 Adam Road, Singapore

Director of program Rev. Derek Tan, Academic Dean

Teaching staff 4 Western - 4 with cross-cultural experience
7non-Western - 5 with cross-cultural experience

Languages of instruction English

Learning styles 80% formal class-room teaching
20% non-formal learning experiences

Courses offered Missiology degree at master's level
World Mission courses in bachelor's degree
World Mission courses at certificate or diploma level

Training ethos Theological Centre for Asia integrates contemporary expeience, classical scholarship and Christian spiritualiy for the equipping and mentoring of men and women for ministry in the church, mission field or market place.

*Contemporary Experience
Faculty and students are involved in the "now" of ministry in churches and on the mission fields.

* Classical Scholarship
Students receive solid biblical, theological and missiological foundations for effective ministry in the real world of today and tomorrow.

*Christian Spirituality
Prayer, worship and fasting are built into the lives of the learning community at TCA.

Profile no. 181   South Africa

Established 1985
AFRICA SCHOOL OF MISSIONS

Mailing address AFRICA SCHOOL OF MISSIONS
P O Box 439 White River
1240 Eastern Transvaal SOUTH AFRICA

Phone 27- 32341   **Fax** 27- 51340

Location   as above

Director of program Rev. G. P. Malan, Principal

Teaching staff   4 Western - none with cross-cultural experience
10 non-Western - 5 with cross-cultural experience

Languages of instruction English

Learning styles 60% formal class-room teaching
40% non-formal learning experiences

Courses offered World Mission courses at diploma level - 3 years
Pre-field training & orientation courses - 1 year

Training ethos A.S.M. serves the Body of Christ as a Spiritual Technicon, offering an excellent academic programme combined with "hands on" practical experience.

Our courses allow the student to major in one of the follwing areas : Missions; Pastoral; French ministry; Health; Urban Missions; and Bible Translation.

Profile no. 182 **South Africa**

Established 1980
EVANGELICAL BIBLE SEMINARY OF SOUTH AFRICA

Mailing address EVANGELICAL BIBLE SEMINARY of
SOUTH AFRICA
P O Box 2400
Pietermaritzburg 3200 SOUTH AFRICA

Phone 27- 331 941 679   **Fax** 27- 331 940 034

Location as above

Director of program Moshe Rajuili, Principal

Teaching staff all staff are nationals - of whatever race

Languages of instruction English

Learning styles 80% formal class-room teaching
20% non-formal learning experiences

Courses offered World Mission courses in bachelor's degree
World Mission courses at certificate or diploma level

Training ethos Ours is a multi-racial, interdenominational mature student body.

The curriculum is based on evangelical convictions, a contextual approach and with missiology as the integrating core.

Academic standards are maintained (head), fieldwork is required (hands) and personal growth is encouraged (heart).

Profile no. 183   South Africa

Established 1986
OPERATION MOBILISATION TRAINING CENTRE

Mailing address OM TRAINING CENTRE
P O Box 30221, Sunnyside
Pretoria 0132 SOUTH AFRICA

Phone 27- 12 911 0316   **Fax** 27- 12 333 2169

Location as above

Director of program Marius Genis, Training Director

Teaching staff 5 Western - 4 with cross-cultural experience
2 non-Western - 2 with cross-cultural experience

Languages of instruction English

Learning styles 50% formal class-room teaching
50% non-formal learning experiences

Courses offered Pre-field training & orientation - 6 & 12 months

Training ethos Our aim is to send "whole" people into the whole world; whole people being those that are spiritually, physically and emotionally ready to be an ambassador for Christ.

Profile no. 184   South Africa

Established 1973
ROSEBANK BIBLE COLLEGE

Mailing address   ROSEBANK BIBLE COLLEGE
PO Box 52047
Saxonwold 2132 SOUTH AFRICA

Phone 27-11 788 5410   **Fax**

Location   corner Cradock & Bierman Ave., Rosebank

Director of program   Dr. R.G. Mathie, Principal

Teaching staff   1 Western - with cross-cultural experience
0 non-Western

Languages of instruction   English

Learning styles   67% formal class-room teaching
33% non-formal learning experiences

Courses offered   World Mission courses in bachelor's degree
World Mission courses at certificate or diploma level

Training ethos   Rosebank Bible College offers residential and distance training.

It represents an evangelical, church-based, world-faced composite of study, committed to the authority of the Scriptures, to academic and spiritual excellence and renewal.

The College is proud of its several routes of study of varying duration (1 to 3 years) which have been used by churches and mission agencies over the last two decades.

There are part-time missiology staff in addition to the one full-time staff member listed above.

Profile no. 185   Spain

Established 1988
PROJECTO MAGREB,
CURSO DE ORIENTACION TRANSCULTURAL

Mailing address PROJECTO MAGREB
Curso de Orientacion Transcultural
Apdo 573
Granada 18080 SPAIN

Phone 34-58 124 133   **Fax** 34-58 124 133

Location In South Spain and several Muslim countries

Director of program Marcos Amado, Training Director

Teaching staff

Languages of instruction Spanish

Learning styles 35% formal class-room teaching
65% non-formal learning experiences

Courses offered Pre-field training & orientation - 4 - 5 months

Training ethos The training is done on the field,

Our goal is to help the missionary in the process of adapting to a new culture.

To reach this purpose, we give classes on anthropology and from the first day in the new country, the worker is put in practical situations - live with Muslim families, travel around the country in public transport, LAMP method etc)

Profile no. 186   Sri Lanka

Established 1970
LANKA BIBLE COLLEGE

Mailing address   LANKA BIBLE COLLEGE
P O Box 2
Peradeniya SRI LANKA

Phone 94-8 88398   **Fax** 94-8 32573

Location   as above

Director of program   Ben Manickam, Principal

Teaching staff   0 Western
15 non-Western - 15 with cross-cultural experience

Languages of instruction   English, Sinhala & Tamil

Learning styles   65% formal class-room teaching
35% non-formal learning experiences

Courses offered   World Mission courses in bachelor's degree
World Mission courses at certificate or diploma level
Pre-field training & orientation courses - 1 yr , 2 yrs.

Training ethos   (a) To provide students with a working knowledge of the word of God through a systematic program of instruction; having the Bible as its centre, principal content & norm.

(b) To equip students in skills needed to bring in the harvest of Christ   & establish an ongoing Christian presence in these locations.

Profile no. 187   Sweden

Established 1919
MISSIONSSKOLA OCH BIBELINSTITUT

Mailing address MISSIONSSKOLA och BIBELINSTITUT
Swedish Alliance Mission
S-55594 Jonköping SWEDEN

Phone 46-36 37 92 05   **Fax** 46-36 379 041

Location as above

Director of program Ingemar Karlsson, Rektor

Teaching staff 5 Western - 2 with cross-cultural experience
0 non-Western

Languages of instruction Swedish

Learning styles 90% formal class-room teaching
10% non-formal learning experiences

Courses offered

Training ethos We train future pastors and missionaries primarily within the Swedish Alliance Mission, SAM.

It is a four year training programme and aims at training students in the languages, other subjects common for a seminary as well as internship programs in various churches.

Profile no. 188   Sweden

Established 1908
ÖREBRO THEOLOGICAL SEMINARY

Mailing address   ÖREBRO THEOLOGICAL SEMINARY
The Mission Institute , Box 1623,
S- 701 16 Örebro SWEDEN

Phone 46-19 11 93 60   **Fax** 46-19 33 27 09

Location   Astadalsvägen 2, Örebro

Director of program   Göran Janzon, Director

Teaching staff   17 Western - 10 with cross-cultural experience
0 non-Western

Languages of instruction   Swedish

Learning styles   75% formal class-room teaching
25% non-formal learning experiences

Courses offered   World Mission courses in bachelor's degree
World Mission courses at certificate or diploma level
Pre-field training & orientation - 1 term of 5 months

Training ethos   The Mission Institute is a course meant to aid those on their way to mission fields.

The term gives the possibility of broadening one's understanding of mission work, and refining one's perception in the role of a missionary.

The training prepares for work, which relztes to an indigenous church in a different society and in another culture and for the encounter with other religions.

Profile no. 189   Switzerland

Established 1970
UNIVERSITY OF THE NATIONS (YWAM) LAUSANNE CENTER

Mailing address JEUNESSE EN MISSION (YWAM)

1000 Lausanne 25 SWITZERLAND

Phone 41-21 784 2325   **Fax** 41-21 784 2320

Location at Chalêt-à-Gobret above Lausanne

Director of program Thomas A. Bloomer

Teaching staff Numerous visiting teachers, all with cross-cultural experience

Languages of instruction English & French

Learning styles 30% formal class-room teaching
70% non-formal learning experiences

Courses offered Missiology degree at master's level
World Mission courses in bachelor's degree
World Mission courses at diploma or certificate level
Pre-field training & orientation - 5 mths to 2 years

Training ethos The University of the Nations is a de-centralized, inter-denominational, cross-cultural missions training structure consisting of 200 training centres operating in 80 countries, teaching in 30 languages.

Profile no. 190 Tonga

Established 1991
TONGA BIBLE COLLEGE

Mailing address TONGA BIBLE COLLEGE
P O Box 2462
Nuku'alofa TONGA

Phone 676 - 23 992   **Fax** 676 - 23 992

Location as above

Director of program Dr Willis C Newman, Principal

Teaching staff 5 Western - all with cross-cultural experience
1 non-Western - with cross-cultural experience

Languages of instruction English & Tongan

Learning styles 100% formal class-room teaching

Courses offered World Mission courses in bachelor's degree
World Mission courses at diploma or certificate level

Training ethos We offer a broad-based education with a balanced mix of academic studies and practical ministry skills.

We stress missions and evangelism grounded on a solid evangelical theological foundation.

Other strengths are in the area of apologetics and creation science.

Profile no. 191   **Ukraine**

Established 1991
DONETSK BIBLE COLLEGE

Mailing address   DONETSK BIBLE COLLEGE
106-a Ilyitcha Prospekt
Donetsk UKRAINE 340 059

Phone 7-622 944 069   **Fax** 7-622 357 046

Location   as above

Director of program   Alexei Melnichuk

Teaching staff   3 Western - 2 with cross-cultural experience
2 non-Western - 2 with cross-cultural experience

Languages of instruction   Russian

Learning styles   80% formal class-room teaching
20% non-formal learning experiences

Courses offered   World Mission courses in bachelor's degree
World Mission courses at certificate or diploma level

Training ethos   With a curriculum that includes much in the area of practical ministry skills, we equip students from the various republics of the Commonwealth of Independent States for effective evangelism, church planting, and discipleship among Slavs, tribal peoples, Muslims and Buddhists.

Profile no. 192   United Kingdom

Established 1964
ALL NATIONS CHRISTIAN COLLEGE

Mailing address   ALL NATIONS CHRISTIAN COLLEGE
Easneye
Ware, Herts.   SG12 8LX ENGLAND, U.K.

Phone 44-920 461 243   **Fax** 44-920 462 997

Location   as above

Director of program   Rev.Dr.C.J.H. Wright, Principal

Teaching staff   17 Western - 15 with cross-cultural experience
1 non-Western & 2 visiting lecturers each year

Languages of instruction   English

Learning styles   70% formal class-room teaching
30% non-formal learning experiences

Courses offered   MA in Missiology
BA in Biblical & Cross-cultural Studies
Diploma in Biblical & Cross-cultural Studies

Training ethos   ANCC emphasises wholistic training, spiritual, academic and practical.

It insists on wives and husbands training together and provides nursery facilities to enable this.

It is multi-cultural (approximately 45% of students being non-British) and multi-denominational.
As well as the course offerings listed above, there is the possibility of doctoral research.

Profile no. 193 United Kingdom

Established
BELFAST BIBLE COLLEGE

Mailing address BELFAST BIBLE COLLEGE
Glenburn House, Glenburn Road South
Dunmurry
Belfast BT17 9JP   NORTHERN IRELAND, U.K.

Phone 44-232 301 551   **Fax**

Location as above

Director of program Rev. Graham Cheesman, Principal

Teaching staff 6 Western - 6 with cross-cultural experience
0 non-Western

Languages of instruction English

Learning styles 90% formal class-room teaching
10% non-formal learning experiences

Courses offered World Mission courses in bachelor's degree
World Mission courses at certificate or diploma level
Pre-field training & orientation - 3 months - 3 years

Training ethos We are a warm community of about 100 students from 20 different countries.

Our aim is to prepare men and women of varying academic abilities for mission, by helping them grow in academic understanding of the Word of God, practical ministry skills and spiritual life.

Profile no. 194　　　　　　　　　　　　　　　United Kingdom

Established 1953
BIRMINGHAM BIBLE INSTITUTE

Mailing address　BIRMINGHAM BIBLE INSTITUTE
5 Pakenham Rd., Edgbaston

Birmingham B15 2NN ENGLAND, U.K.

Phone　44-21 440 4016　　**Fax**

Location　centre of city

Director of program　Mark Beaumont, Mission Studies

Teaching staff　6 Western - 1 with cross-cultural experience
0 non-Western

Languages of instruction　English

Learning styles　75% formal class-room teaching
25% non-formal learning experiences

Courses offered　World Mission courses at certificate or diploma level

Training ethos　The use of the multi-ethnic situation of Birmingham for cross-cultural training.

An emphasis on the spiritual/devotional life of the student
as well as the biblical/academic.

Profile no. 195 United Kingdom

Established 1985
CAREY COLLEGE

Mailing address CAREY COLLEGE
PO Box 1002, Bawtry
Doncaster, S Yorkshire DN10 6SP ENGLAND, U.K.

Phone 44-302 710 020   **Fax** 44-302 710 027

Location Bawtry Hall, Bawtry

Director of program Mr. S.D. Bell, Director

Teaching staff 1 Western - 1 with cross-cultural experience
0 non-Western

Languages of instruction English

Learning styles 0% formal class-room teaching
100% non-formal learning experiences

Courses offered Pre-field training & orientation - 3 courses - flexible time

Training ethos Distance - learning programme on Islam & Christian witness, to prepare Christians for friendship evangelism.

Flexible time scale for courses. 21 study topics.

Profile no. 196   United Kingdom

Established 1993
CONWY HOUSE TRAINING CENTRE

Mailing address   CONWY HOUSE TRAINING CENTRE
115 Russell Road
Rhyl, Clwyd   LL18 4ED WALES, U.K.

Phone 44-7445 343 085   **Fax** 44- 745 330790

Location   as above

Director of program   Ian Orton

Teaching staff   20 Western - 18 with cross-cultural experience
0 non-Western

Languages of instruction   English

Learning styles   70% formal class-room teaching
30% non-formal learning experiences

Courses offered   Pre-field training & orientation - 5, 6 & 8weeks

Training ethos   The Language School offers courses in English as a Foreign Language to those entering missions and needing English for international communication.

Teaching includes formal language study and orientation for personal spiritual life as well as missions orientation and cross-cultural evangelism.

Profile no. 197 United Kingdom

Established 1969
CROWTHER HALL

Mailing address CROWTHER HALL
Weoley Park Rd
Selly Oak
Birmingham   B29 6QT ENGLAND, U.K.

Phone 44-21 472 4228   **Fax** 44-21 471 2662

Location as above

Director of program Rev. Colin G. Chapman, Principal

Teaching staff 4 Western - 4 with cross-cultural experience
0 non-Western

Languages of instruction English

Learning styles 75% formal class-room teaching
25% non-formal learning experiences

Courses offered Missiology degree at doctoral level
Missiology degree at master's level
World Mission courses at certificate or diploma level
Pre-field training & orientation - 1, 2 or 3 terms of 11wks

Training ethos A small college of 36 students plus staff and families - approximately half from the UK, preparing to go overseas and the other half from overseas.

This creates a unique context for training in which there is a strong emphasis on personal and spiritual formation.

We are fully involved in the Department of Mission in the Selly Oak Colleges and through them with the University of Birmingham. The multi-faith and multi-cultural areas of inner city Birmingham provide an excellent setting for action- reflection training.

We try to provide training that is "tailor-made" for each individual.

Profile no. 198 United Kingdom

Established 1925
ELIM BIBLE COLLEGE

Mailing address ELIM BIBLE COLLEGE
1,The Grove,London Road
Nantwich, Cheshire   CW5 6LW ENGLAND, U.K.

Phone 44-270 610 800   **Fax** 44-270 610 013

Location as above

Director of program J.C. Smyth, Principal

Teaching staff 6 Western - 2 with cross-cultural experience
0 non-Western

Languages of instruction English

Learning styles 60% formal class-room teaching
40% non-formal learning experiences

Courses offered World Mission courses in bachelor's degree
World Mission courses at certificate or diploma level
Pre-field training & orientation - 3 months per annum

Training ethos The courses offered lead to a nationally validated BA degree and provide valuable field experience in areas chosen by the student as a part of the degree course.

Profile no. 199　　　　　　　　　　　　　　　　United Kingdom

Established
EMMANUEL BIBLE COLLEGE

Mailing address　EMMANUEL BIBLE COLLEGE
1 Palm Grove
Birkenhead, Merseyside L43 1TE ENGLAND, U.K.

Phone 44-51 642 23412　　**Fax**

Location　as above

Director of program　Rev.Vic. Edwards, Principal

Teaching staff　5 Western - 3 with cross-cultural experience
0 non-Western

Languages of instruction　English

Learning styles　80% formal class-room teaching
20% non-formal learning experiences

Courses offered　World Mission courses at certificate or diploma level
Pre-field training & orientation

Training ethos　Emmanuel Bible College is a centre for training Christian men & women to take their places as pragmatic leaders in the service of Christ & His Church.

Emmanuel is interdenominational, evangelical & of Wesleyan heritage.

Underlying the whole training programme is the conviction that Christian commitment, integrity & character development are of first importance!

Profile no. 200   **United Kingdom**

Established
EQUIP

Mailing address   EQUIP
Bawtry Hall
Bawtry, Doncaster   DN10 6JH ENGLAND, U.K.

Phone 44-302 710 020   **Fax** 44-302 710 027

Location   as above

Director of program   Tony Horsfall, Manager

Teaching staff   3 Western - 3 with cross-cultural experience
0 non-Western

Languages of instruction   English

Learning styles   80% formal class-room teaching
20% non-formal learning experiences

Courses offered   Pre-field training & orientation - 2 weeks

Training ethos   Our aim is to prepare Christians for cross-cultural ministry at home and overseas and to provide in-service training for mission personnel.

We also aim to help adults and children with the re-entry process.

Profile no. 201   United Kingdom

Established 1985
EVANGELICAL THEOLOGICAL COLLEGE OF WALES

Mailing address EVANGELICAL THEOLOGICAL COLLEGE
of WALES
Brvntirion House
Bridgend Mid-Glam. CF31 4DX WALES, U.K.

Phone 44-656 645 411   **Fax** 44-656 668 709

Location as above

Director of program Dr.D.Eryl Davies, Principal

Teaching staff

Languages of instruction English

Learning styles 60% formal class-room teaching
40% non-formal learning experiences

Courses offered Missiology degree at doctoral level
Missiology degree at master's level
World Mission courses in bachelor's degree
World Mission courses at certificate or diploma level
Pre-field training & orientation - 3wks UK; 6wks abroad

Training ethos The training is biblical, contemporary and given within a prayerful context in which holiness is emphasised and church involvement.

Profile no. 202　　　　　　　　　　　　　　　　United Kingdom

Established 1892
GLASGOW BIBLE COLLEGE

Mailing address　GLASGOW BIBLE COLLEGE
　　　　　　　　　731 Great Western Road
　　　　　　　　　Glasgow G12 8QX SCOTLAND, U.K.

　　　　　　　　　Phone 44-41 334 9849　　**Fax** 44-41 334 0012

Location　　　centre of Scotland's most multi-ethnic city, close to Asian
　　　　　　　　& Chinese communities and to Glasgow University.

Director of program　Rev Peter White, Principal

Teaching staff　6 Western - 2 with cross-cultural experience
　　　　　　　　0 non-Western but many visiting teachers.

Languages of instruction　English

Learning styles　85% formal class-room teaching
　　　　　　　　15% non-formal learning experiences

Courses offered　World Mission courses in bachelor's degree
　　　　　　　　World Mission courses at certificate or diploma level
　　　　　　　　Pre-field training & orientation - considerale emphasis

Training ethos　Our exciting new degree programme, designed to prepare
　　　　　　　　men and women for effective hands-on ministry has
　　　　　　　　missiology firmly at the heart of both compulsory and
　　　　　　　　elective courses.

　　　　　　　　Students may major in mission studies with
　　　　　　　　opportunities to focus on their chosen field and ministry.

　　　　　　　　A masters degree programme was due to begin in 1994.

Profile no. 203　　　　　　　　　　　　　　　United Kingdom

Established 1990
LUKE TRAINING CENTRE - OPERATION MOBILISATION

Mailing address LUKE TRAINING CENTRE - OPERATION MOBILISATION
Zion. Little Cornbow
Halesowen, W.Midlands B63 3AJ ENGLAND, U.K.

Phone 44- 21 585 5662　　**Fax** 44- 21 585 0271

Location as above

Director of program D.J.S. Harper

Teaching staff 4 Western - 4 with cross-cultural experience
1 non-Western with cross-cultural experience

Languages of instruction English

Learning styles 40% formal class-room teaching
60% non-formal learning experiences

Courses offered Pre-field training & orientation - from 3 wks to 1 year

Training ethos A part of Operation Mobilisation's role "to motivate, develop and equip people for world evangelazation".

Our objective is to take people from a wide variety of national, educational and denominational backgrounds and through biblical and practical training to prepare people for their particular area of service as "World Christians"- within the context of urban, chidren's, youth, Muslim, Hindu, Sikh & other evangelism in the UK.

Profile no. 204   United Kingdom

Established 1948
MOORLANDS COLLEGE

Mailing address   MOORLANDS COLLEGE
Sopley
Christchurch, Dorset   BH23 7AT ENGLAND, U.K.

Phone 44-425 72369   **Fax** 44-425 74162

Location   as above

Director of program   Dr Derek B Copley, Principal

Teaching staff   9 Western - 6 with cross-cultural experience
0 non-Western

Languages of instruction   English

Learning styles   70% formal class-room teaching
30% non-formal learning experiences

Courses offered   World Mission courses at certificate or diploma level

Training ethos   Focus on balance between academic, spiritual & practical.

Emphasis on 'hands on' experience in interdenominational setting.

Material taught with global perspective.

Profile no. 205 United Kingdom

Established 1946
NORTHUMBRIA BIBLE COLLEGE

Mailing address NORTHUMBRIA BIBLE COLLEGE
52 Castle Terrace
Berwick- upon-Tweed TD15 1PA ENGLAND, U.K.

Phone 44-289 306 190   **Fax** 44-289 306 190

Location as above

Director of program Dr. David Smith, Principal

Teaching staff 9 Western - 7 with cross-cultural experience
0 non-Western

Languages of instruction English

Learning styles 60% formal class-room teaching
40% non-formal learning experiences

Courses offered World Mission courses in bachelor's degree
World Mission courses at certificate or diploma level

Training ethos The fundamental principle is to provide a programme which has mission as its central focus.

We have tried to ensure that missiological priorities and questions shape every aspect of the curriculum.

Courses aim to provide both biblical foundations for mission and deep knowledge of contexts within which mission is under taken.

Profile no. 206   United Kingdom

Established 1983
OXFORD CENTRE FOR MISSION STUDIES

Mailing address OXFORD CENTRE for MISSION STUDIES
PO Box 70
Oxford OX2 6HB ENGLAND, U.K.

Phone 44-865 560 71   **Fax** 44-865 510 823

Location St. Philip and St. James Church
Woodstock Road. Oxford

Director of program Rev.Dr.Chris Sugden, Principal

Teaching staff 1 Western - 1 with cross-cultural experience
2 non-Western - 2 with cross-cultural experience

Languages of instruction English

Learning styles Tutorial for individuals
Seminars/ Lectures

Courses offered Missiology degree at doctoral level
Missiology degree at master's level
World Mission courses in bachelor's degree
World Mission courses at certificate or diploma level

Training ethos Our degrees are by extension with the UK Open University requiring six weeks residence in UK per annum for research degrees.

Our Oxford University Certificate in Theology for Development or Communication studies requires 9 months residence in 2 year programme for M.Div. equivalent.

Profile no. 207   United Kingdom

Established 1892
REDCLIFFE COLLEGE

Mailing address REDCLIFFE COLLEGE
Wotton House, Horton Road

Gloucester,Glos. GL1 ENGLAND, U.K.

Phone   **Fax**

Location   as above

Director of program   Victor A S Reid, Principal

Teaching staff   4 Western - 2 with cross-cultural experience
0 non-Western

Languages of instruction   English

Learning styles   67% formal class-room teaching
33% non-formal learning experiences

Courses offered   World Mission courses at certificate or diploma level
Pre-field training & orientation

Training ethos   Redcliffe is involved in training an international body of men and women for Christian service, with a special emphasis on world evangelism and cross-cultural mission, through full-time and part-time courses which vary in length from
7 weeks to 3 years.

A distinctive "field term placement scheme" provides a total of 40 weeks (over 3 years) of structured, practical, Christian work experience for each student in areas of their own choice, relevant to future ministry.

Each student is also encouraged to make progress in their personal and spiritual development.

Profile no. 208   United Kingdom

Established
SELLEY OAK COLLEGES, DEPARTMENT OF MISSION

Mailing address   SELLEY OAK COLLEGES
Department of Mission,
Weolev Park Rd
Selly Oak, Birmingham   B29 6LQ ENGLAND, U.K.

                        Phone   44-21 472 4231   **Fax**   44-21 472 8852

Location   4 miles fromcentre of Birmingham, England's second largest city

Director of program   Rev.J.Andrew Kirk, Dean of Mission

Teaching staff   12 Western - 11 with cross-cultural experience
5 non-Western - 5 with cross-cultural experience

Languages of instruction   English

Learning styles

Courses offered   Missiology degree at masters & doctoral levels
World Mission courses at certificate or diploma level
Pre-field training & orientation - 1, 2 or 3 terms(1year)

Training ethos   The context of education highlights the multi-cultural nature of both sstudents and staff.

                      Recognition is made of the adult, post-experience character of most participants. A balance is struck between teacher input and learner sharing.

                      Flexibility is a hallmark of our programmes.

Profile no. 209   United Kingdom

Established 1989

SOUTHALL SCHOOL OF LANGUAGES & MISSIONARY ORIENTATION

Mailing address   SOUTHALL SCHOOL of Languages & Missionary
Orientation
Western Road
Southall, Middx.   UB2 5DS ENGLAND, U.K.

Phone 44-81 574 4456   **Fax**

Location   Southall Baptist Church

Director of program   Boyd V. Williams, Director

Teaching staff   1 Western - 1 with cross-cultural experience
0 non-Western

Languages of instruction   English

Learning styles   50% formal class-room teaching
50% non-formal learning experiences

Courses offered   Pre-field training & orientation - 6 months & 6 months placement

Training ethos   The school is set in a multi-cultural (mainly Asian) part of Greater London.

Emphasis on learning through living in another culture and
in the context of mission.

Courses may be combined with English studies.

Further emphasis on lower cost with a view to students for developing countries.

Profile no. 210   United Kingdom

Established 1953
SUMMER INSTITUTE OF LINGUISTICS - BRITISH SCHOOL

Mailing address SUMMER INSTITUTE of LINGUISTICS, British School
Horsleys Green
High Wycombe, Bucks. HP14 3XL ENGLAND, U.K.

Phone 44- 494 482 521   **Fax** 44- 494 483 297

Location as above

Director of program Dr. David H. Crozier

Teaching staff Western - with cross-cultural experience
non-Western - with cross-cultural experience

Languages of instruction English

Learning styles 30% formal class-room teaching
70% non-formal learning experiences

Courses offered Pre-field training & orientation - 2 to 40 weeks

Training ethos Intensive courses in language and culture learning, linguistic analysis, literacy, anthropology and translation for those going overseas.

Profile no. 211 United Kingdom

Established 1993
THE MISSIONARY TRAINING SERVICE

Mailing address THE MISSIONARY TRAINING SERVICE
Oswestry Christian Centre, Lower Brook Street
Oswestry, Shropshire SY11 2XY ENGLAND, U.K.

Phone 44- 691 653 619   **Fax** 44- 691 653 619

Location as above

Director of program Rev.Ian E. Benson, Co-ordinator

Teaching staff 4 Western - 4 with cross-cultural experience
0 non-Western

Languages of instruction English, Spanish, French, Thai

Learning styles

Courses offered Pre-field training & orientation - 3 months to 3 years

Training ethos Missionary candidates learn on-the-job, in a church context, under personal guidance and supervision, how to plant churches, and also multiply them by training new leaders behind the scenes.

By God's grace, the training programmes aim to multiply local churches and groups whilst preparing missionaries in reproducible methods for the field, especially the remaining unreached peoples.

Teaching and practice run parallel. All teaching is related to and flows from practice in planting churches and training others.

Profile no. 212 United Kingdom

Established 1971
TRINITY COLLEGE

Mailing address   TRINITY COLLEGE
24 Stoke Hill
Bristol, Avon   BS9 1JP ENGLAND, U.K.

Phone 44- 272 682 803   **Fax** 44- 272 687 470

Location   as above

Director of program   Rev Howard Peskett, Tutor

Teaching staff   12 Western - 1 with cross-cultural experience
1 non-Western with cross-cultural experience

Languages of instruction   English

Learning styles   75% formal class-room teaching
25% non-formal learning experiences

Courses offered   Missiology degree at master's level
World Mission courses in bachelor's degree
World Mission courses at certificate or diploma level

Training ethos   Trinity is an Anglican Theological College with 1/3 non-Anglican students.

Usually 10 - 15 international students.

Primary focus is UK mission.

Profile no. 213 United Kingdom

Established 1978
TURNING POINT TRAINING CENTRE (OM)

Mailing address TURNING POINT TRAINING CENTRE, Operation
Mobilisation
134 Gordon Road. West Ealing
London W13 8PJ ENGLAND, U.K.

Phone 44-81 991 1332   **Fax** 44-81 998 8810

Location as above

Director of program Randy Lawler, Field leader

Teaching staff 8 Western - 8 with cross-cultural experience
2 non-Western - 2 with cross-cultural experience

Languages of instruction English

Learning styles 33% formal class-room teaching
66% non-formal learning experiences

Courses offered Pre-field training & orientation - 1 & 2 years

Training ethos OM Turning Point, a ministry of Operation Mobilisation, located in London. It offers practical, hands-on training in Muslim evangelism together with the basic OM discipleship training.

In this training course, you will be challenged towards building a better relationship with God, learning cross-cultural & inter-personal skills and learning to share your faith with everyone and then more specifically with Muslims. Muslim students, Arabs, Turks, Kurds and Iranians are our main target people groups.

The course will involve studies, book reading, discussions and practical training in basic Christian discipleship, evangelism, leadership, Islamics and Middle Eastern languages.

Short-term intensive English courses are offered for

Profile no. 214 United States Of America

Established 1973
AGAPE INTERNATIONAL TRAINING
CAMPUS CRUSADE

Mailing address AGAPE INTERNATIONAL TRAINING,
Campus Crusade
PO Box 10389
Bakersfield CA 93309 USA

Phone (805) 861 1043   **Fax** (805) 861 1302

Location 1225 California Avenue, Bakersfield

Director of program Bob Doozan, Director

Teaching staff 24 Western - 17 with cross-cultural experience
0 non-Western

Languages of instruction English

Learning styles 25% formal class-room teaching
75% non-formal learning experiences

Courses offered Pre-field training & orientation - 11 weeks

Training ethos This is an "internship" training.

Classroom time is highly "interactive".

General training is largely "experiential"

One shepherd to 4 missionary candidates - the shepherd is a "mentor", facilitator, encourager, not one who must have all the answers.

Profile no. 215 United States Of America

Established 1966
ALASKA BIBLE COLLEGE

Mailing address   ALASKA BIBLE COLLEGE
Box 289
Glennallen, AK   99588 USA

Phone (907) 822-3201   **Fax** (907) 822-5027

Location   south-central Alaska,
190 miles north-east of Anchorage

Director of program   Virgil Ball. Missions Coordinator

Teaching staff   4 Western - 3 with cross-cultural experience
0 non-Western

Languages of instruction   English

Learning styles   90% formal class-room teaching
10% non-formal learning experiences

Courses offered   World Mission courses in bachelor's degree

Training ethos   Classroom instruction is augmented by opportunities for involvement in outreach in a missions setting.

A missions internship is required for all second major missions students.

Profile no. 216   United States Of America

Established
AMOR MINISTRIES

Mailing address   AMOR MINISTRIES
1664 Precision Park Lane
San Diego, CA 92115 USA

Phone (619) 662 1200   **Fax** (619) 662 1295

Location   as above

Director of program   Scott Congdon, President

Teaching staff   4 Western - 3 with cross-cultural experience
0 non-Western

Languages of instruction   English

Learning styles

Courses offered   Pre-field training & orientation - 5 days

Training ethos

Profile no. 217   United States Of America

Established 1971
ARIZONA COLLEGE OF THE BIBLE

Mailing address   ARIZONA COLLEGE of the BIBLE
Department of Cross-Cultural Studies
2045 W. Northern Ave
Phoenix, AZ   85021 USA

Phone (602) 995-2670   **Fax**

Location   as above

Director of program   Lester J. Hirst, Chair.

Teaching staff   1 Western - 1 with cross-cultural experience
0 non-Western

Languages of instruction   English (Spanish available)

Learning styles   60% formal class-room teaching
40% non-formal learning experiences

Courses offered   World Mission courses in bachelor's degree
World Mission courses at certificate or diploma level

Training ethos   We have a strong emphasis on character building.

Internship experiences are supervised to optimize learning.

Many cross-cultural experiences available in the Phoenix vicinity.

Strong emphasis on those going to Latin America or to Latinos.

Profile no. 218 United States Of America

Established 1993
AZUSA PACIFIC UNIVERSITY, GLOBAL STUDIES PROGRAM

Mailing address AZUSA PACIFIC UNIVERSITY
Global Studies Program
901 E. Alosta Ave.
Azusa, CA 91702 USA

Phone (818) 969 3434   **Fax**

Location Los Angeles

Director of program Richard Slimbach, Chair, Global

Teaching staff 3 Western - 3 with cross-cultural experience
2 non-Western - 2 with cross-cultural experience

Languages of instruction

Learning styles 50% formal class-room teaching
50% non-formal learning experiences

Courses offered World Mission courses in bachelor's degree

Training ethos Baccalaureate program integrating formal course work in international politics, world geography, comparative religions, inter-cultural communication, etc. with experiential learning in developing cross-cultural relationships and analyzing urban settings (in Los Angeles), all culminating in a one term study and service practicum in a non-Western (for Western students) field.

Profile no. 219 United States Of America

Established 1970
BAPTIST BIBLE SEMINARY

Mailing address BAPTIST BIBLE SEMINARY
538 Venard Road
Clarks Summit, PA 18411 USA

Phone (717) 586 2400   **Fax** (717) 586 1753

Location as above

Director of program Dr. James King, Director of Missions

Teaching staff 7 Western - 7 with cross-cultural experience
0 non-Western

Languages of instruction English

Learning styles 70% formal class-room teaching
30% non-formal learning experiences

Courses offered Missiology degree at doctoral level
Missiology degree at master's level
World Mission courses in bachelor's degree

Training ethos We have an integrated approach, balancing the academics of a traditional classroom with a required 1 year of internship worth 27 credit hours.

Profile no. 220   United States Of America

Established 1883
BELHAVEN COLLEGE

Mailing address   BELHAVEN COLLEGE
1500 Peach tree Street
Jackson, MS   39202 - 1789 USA

Phone (601) 968 5907   **Fax** (601) 968 9998

Location   as above

Director of program   Rev Dr Joseph M. Martin

Teaching staff   2 Western - 2 with cross-cultural experience
0 non-Western

Languages of instruction   English

Learning styles   90% formal class-room teaching
10% non-formal learning experiences

Courses offered   World Mission courses in bachelor's degree
World Mission courses at certificate or diploma level

Training ethos   1   Emphasis on the Bible as both source of doctrine and model of wholistic cross-cultural mission.

2   Focus on the incarnation of Christ as the supreme model of all types of ministry.

3   Emphasis on reaching the unreached and ministering with the poor.

Profile no. 221   United States Of America

Established 1948
BETHANY COLLEGE OF MISSIONS

Mailing address   BETHANY COLLEGE OF MISSIONS
6820 Auto Club Rd
Minneapolis, MN   55438 USA

Phone (612) 944 2121   **Fax** (612) 829 2535

Location   as above

Director of program   Patrick Krayer, Dean

Teaching staff   13 Western - 9 with cross-cultural experience
1 non-Western with cross-cultural experience

Languages of instruction   English

Learning styles   50% formal class-room teaching
50% non-formal learning experiences

Courses offered   Bachelor's degree in Cross-cultural Studies

Training ethos   The purpose of Bethany College of Missions is to prepare men and women to be cross-cultural missionaries.

This is accomplished through a unique blend of classroom study, ministry training and practical training.

Aviation program also available.

Profile no. 222   **United States Of America**

Established 1947
BETHEL COLLEGE (INDIANA)

Mailing address   BETHEL COLLEGE
1001 W. McKinley Ave
Mishawaka, IN   46545 USA

Phone (219) 257 3378   **Fax** (219) 257 3326

Location   north-central Indiana, 2 hours from down-town Chicago
5 minutes from University of Notre Dame

Director of program   Dr Laverne Blowers

Teaching staff   6 Western - 5 with cross-cultural experience
0 non-Western

Languages of instruction   English

Learning styles   80% formal class-room teaching
20% non-formal learning experiences

Courses offered   World Mission courses in bachelor's degree

Training ethos   Bethel College is an evangelical Christian liberal arts college affiliated with the Missionary Church.

As a co-educational college it offers studies for career and personal growth ranging from masters, baccalaureate and associate degrees, to non-degree programs for the broad spectrum of students.

Profile no. 223   United States Of America

Established 1992
CALVIN MISSIONS INSTITUTE

Mailing address CALVIN MISSIONS INSTITUTE
3233 Burton Street S.E.
Grand Rapids, MI 49546 USA

Phone (616) 957-6036   **Fax** (616) 957-8621

Location as above

Director of program Dr Roger S Greenway

Teaching staff 4 Western - 3 with cross-cultural experience
0 non-Western

Languages of instruction English , Portuguese & Spanish

Learning styles 80% formal class-room teaching
20% non-formal learning experiences

Courses offered Missiology degree at master's level
Pre-field training & orientation - 1 week intensive

Training ethos The Missions Institute offers a variety of seminars and workshops, formal and non-formal, on the USA campus and in other countries, addressing the issues and needs of missionaries and church pastors working in their own culture or cross-culturally and drawing upon the teaching resources of specialists in various fields.

Overall goal: Enhance the spread of the gospel and church planting.

Profile no. 224   United States Of America

Established 1953
CEDARVILLE COLLEGE

Mailing address   CEDARVILLE COLLEGE
PO Box 601
Cedarville, OH   45314 USA

Phone (513) 766 - 2211   **Fax** (513) 766-2760

Location   256 N. Main Street, Cedarville

Director of program   Dr. Floyd S Elmore

Teaching staff   2 Western - 2 with cross-cultural experience
0 non-Western

Languages of instruction   English

Learning styles   75% formal class-room teaching
25% non-formal learning experiences

Courses offered   World Mission courses in bachelor's degree

Training ethos   TWO TRACKS:

1) Bible comprehensive - MISSIONS:
includes 30 quarter hours of missions and 60 quarter hours of Bible ezposition and THEOLOGY. Cross-cultural internship required.

2) International Studies - MISSIOLOGY:
Includes, along with Missions, specific courses studies in International Business, Economics, Political Science, World literature and philosophy, Geopraphy and Sociology designed for the tentmaker missionary.

Profile no. 225   United States Of America

Established 1975
CHURCH OF GOD SCHOOL OF THEOLOGY

Mailing address   CHURCH OF GOD SCHOOL of THEOLOGY
Missiology Program
PO Box 3330
Cleveland TN   37320 - 3330 USA

Phone (615) 478 1131   **Fax** (615) 478 7155

Location

Director of program   Dr Grant McClung, Missiology Program

Teaching staff   15 Western - half with cross-cultural experience
2 non-Western - 2 with cross-cultural experience

Languages of instruction   English

Learning styles   75% formal class-room teaching
25% non-formal learning experiences

Courses offered   Missiology degree at master's level

Training ethos

Profile no. 226   United States Of America

Established 1923
COLUMBIA INTERNATIONAL UNIVERSITY

Mailing address   COLUMBIA INTERNATIONAL UNIVERSITY
PO Box 3122
Columbia, SC   29230   USA

Phone (803) 754 - 4100   **Fax** (803) 786 - 4209

Location

Director of program   Dr. Johnny Miller, President

Teaching staff   51   Western - 19 with cross-cultural experience
1 non-Western with cross-cultural experience

Languages of instruction   English

Learning styles   92% formal class-room teaching
8% non-formal learning experiences

Courses offered   Missiology degree at doctoral level
Missiology degree at master's level
World Mission courses in bachelor's degree

Training ethos   Columbia International University offers missionary training at all levels through semesterized and intensive (1-3 week) modular classes on campus, through extension sites in the USA and Germany and through independent distance learning.

Columbia is firmly committed to the authority of scripture, to holiness of life and to world evangeli ation.

Profile no. 227 United States Of America

Established 1983
CONCORDIA COLLEGE
OSWALD HOFFMAN SCHOOL OF OUTREACH

Mailing address   CONCORDIA COLLEGE
Oswald Hoffman School of Outreach
275 N. Svndicate
St Paul, MN   55104 USA

        Phone (612) 641 - 8830   **Fax** (612) 459 - 0207

Location   as above

Director of program   Dr. Richard Carter, Director

Teaching staff   4 Western - 3 with cross-cultural experience
1 non-Western - 1 with cross-cultural experience

Languages of instruction   English

Learning styles   85% formal class-room teaching
15% non-formal learning experiences

Courses offered   World Mission courses in bachelor's degree

Training ethos   OHSCO is dedicated to equipping professional church workers and lay persons for outreach.

Through residential/non-residential training students are equipped for mission contexts - whether it be cross-cultural or mono-cultural contexts.

Spiritual formation is the foundation upon which in-ministry experiences and classroom knowledge is reflected upon to holistically equip for mission.

Profile no. 228   United States Of America

Established 1924
DALLAS THEOLOGICAL SEMINARY

Mailing address   DALLAS THEOLOGICAL SEMINARY
Department of World Missions
3909 Swiss Ave
Dallas, TX   75204 USA

Phone (214) 824 3094   **Fax** (214) 841 3664

Location   as above

Director of program   Dr. Michael Pocock, Chairman

Teaching staff   2 Western - 2 with cross-cultural experience
1 non-Western with cross-cultural experience

Languages of instruction   English

Learning styles   80% formal class-room teaching
20% non-formal learning experiences

Courses offered   Missiology degree at master's level
World Mission courses at diploma or certificate level

Training ethos   Biblical and theological studies form the heart of missionary preparation at DTS. Missiology is taught and evaluated through the lens of Scripture.

Graduates often teach the Bible and theology in cross-cultural settings as well as planting churches.

In addition to MA and ThM with missions emphasis, missionaries may pursue D.Min. or Ph.D. in Bible/theology.

Profile no. 229											United States Of America

Established 1950
DENVER SEMINARY

Mailing address   DENVER SEMINARY
Department of World Christianity
P O Box 10.000
Denver CO 80250 USA

Phone (303) 761 2482   **Fax** (303) 761 8060

Location   1913 S Michigan Way

Director of program   The Dean

Teaching staff   3 Western - 3 with cross-cultural experience
0 non-Western

Languages of instruction   English

Learning styles   80% formal class-room teaching
20% non-formal learning experiences

Courses offered   Missiology degree at doctoral level

Training ethos   We equip both prospective and experienced missionaries for effective cross-cultural ministry.

We give nationals from other lands tools to help them minister more effectively in their own contexts.

And we assist those who intend to remain in North America to become more culturally sensitive and to be able to minister with competence among people of diverse backgrounds.

Profile no. 230   United States Of America

Established 1984
EASTERN COLLEGE

Mailing address   EASTERN COLLEGE
Economic Development
10 Fairview Drive
St. Davids, PA 19087 - 3696 USA

Phone (215) 341 5972   **Fax** (215) 341 1466

Location   as above

Director of program   W. Ward Gasque, Dean

Teaching staff   36 Western - 15 with cross-cultural experience
3 non-Western - 3 with cross-cultural experience

Languages of instruction   English

Learning styles   100% formal class-room teaching

Courses offered   Missiology degree at master's level

Training ethos   Holistic missions focused on developing small businesses to create economic opportunities for those in poverty.

Eastern College provides training for Christians desiring to work in the field of Economic Development. Students are required to complete a four months internship, often with Christian development organizarions in the Philadelphia area, across the U.S. and arouns the world.

Two concentration areas exist : Urban and Global. The program, which awards a Master of Busiiness Administration or Master of Science degree emphasizes small-scale entrepreneurial ventures and initiatives designed to empower the poor.

A dual degree program offering the Master of Divinity along with the above options is available jointly with Eastern Baptist Theological Seminary.

Profile no. 231   United States Of America

Established 1941
EMMAUS BIBLE COLLEGE

Mailing address   EMMAUS BIBLE COLLEGE
2570 Asbury Road
Dubuque, IA   52001   USA

Phone (319) 588 8000   **Fax** (319) 588 1216

Location   as above

Director of program   Prof. Kenneth C. Fleming

Teaching staff   10 Western - 2 with cross-cultural experience
0 non-Western

Languages of instruction   English

Learning styles   100% formal class-room teaching

Courses offered   World Mission courses in bachelor's degree
World Mission courses at certificate or diploma level

Training ethos   Emmaus provides a traditional approach to missions through classroom and cross-cultural experience.

Profile no. 232　　　　　　　　　　　United States Of America

Established 1984
ESCUELA DE MISIONES BETANIA

Mailing address　ESCUELA DE MISIONES BETANIA
Calle 13 S. O. # 824
Caparra Terrace, PR 00921 PUERTO RICO , USA

Phone (809) 782 5152　　**Fax** (809) 781 7986

Location　San Juan, P.Rico

Director of program　Carmen Roldan, Dean

Teaching staff　0 Western
8 non-Western - 4 with cross-cultural experience

Languages of instruction　Spanish

Learning styles　100% formal class-room teaching

Courses offered　World Mission courses at certificate or diploma level

Training ethos　Our program is a 10 course night program with the purpose
of preparing Puerto Ricans (through courses on Bible & Missions) for serving as global Christians, either through being senders or goers.

For those who so choose, the EMB acknowledges & gives extra credit to those who do a year's internship in a cross-cultural setting with a recognized mission.

Profile no. 233 United States Of America

Established 1925
EUGENE BIBLE COLLEGE

Mailing address EUGENE BIBLE COLLEGE
2155 Bailey Hill Road
Eugene, OR 97405 USA

Phone (503) 485 1780 **Fax**

Location as above

Director of program Clayton Crymes, Academic Dean

Teaching staff 1 Western - 1 with cross-cultural experience
0 non-Western

Languages of instruction English

Learning styles 99% formal class-room teaching

Courses offered World Mission courses in bachelor's degree

Training ethos Our program is aimed at general missionary preparation oriented toward practical considerations for success on the field. Focus is not on missiology as a theoretical entity.

Profile no. 234 United States Of America

Established
FAITH BAPTIST BIBLE COLLEGE & SEMINARY

Mailing address FAITH BAPTIST BIBLE COLLEGE & SEMINARY Dept. of
World Missions
1900 N.W. 4th Street
Ankeny, IA 50021 USA

Phone (515) 964 0601   **Fax** (515) 964 1638

Location

Director of program   Earl J Danneberg

Teaching staff   26 Western - 13 with cross-cultural experience
1 non-Western - with cross-cultural experience

Languages of instruction   English

Learning styles

Courses offered   World Mission courses in bachelor's degree

Training ethos

Profile no. 235 — United States Of America

Established 1969
FAITH EVANGELICAL LUTHERAN SEMINARY

Mailing address FAITH EVANGELICAL LUTHERAN SEMINARY
P O Box 7186
Tacoma, WA. 98407 USA

Phone (206) 752 2020   **Fax** (206) 759 1790

Location 3504 North Pearl Street, Tacoma

Director of program Dr Ray Arnold

Teaching staff 4 Western - all with cross-cultural experience
1 non-Western - with cross-cultural experience

Languages of instruction English

Learning styles 100% formal class-room teaching - based on practical, cross-cultural experience

Courses offered Missiology degree at doctoral level
Missiology degree at master's level

Training ethos Our approach could be characterized as academic with a strong practical emphasis.

Our approach could also be characterized as professional as opposed to academic research.

We encourage academic excellence but all teaching is done from cross-cultural experience. All of our professors have had cross-cultural experience. Our non-Western professor (Korean) received the majority of his education in Korea.

Profile no. 236 United States Of America

Established 1942
FREE WILL BAPTIST BIBLE COLLEGE

Mailing address FREEWILL BAPTIST BIBLE COLLEGE
3606 West End Avenue
Nashville, TN   37205 USA

Phone (615) 383 1340   **Fax** (615) 269 6028

Location as above

Director of program Acting Director

Teaching staff 2 Western - 2 with cross-cultural experience
0 non-Western

Languages of instruction English

Learning styles 90% formal class-room teaching
10% non-formal learning experiences

Courses offered World Mission courses in bachelor's degree

Training ethos A basic Bible college approach offering a 40 hour Bible major and 25 hour mission track.

Included with the class-room experience are inter-cultural practical ministry opportunities to internationals studying English (conversation partner); teaching English to refugees; and similar cross-cultural experiences.

Profile no. 237   United States Of America

Established 1965
FULLER THEOLOGICAL SEMINARY, SCHOOL OF WORLD MISSION

Mailing address   FULLER THEOLOGICAL SEMINARY
School of World Mission
135 N. Oakland Avenue
Pasadena, CA   91182 USA

Phone (818) 584 - 5260   **Fax** (818) 449 - 5073

Location   as above

Director of program   Dr. J. Dudley Woodberry, Dean

Teaching staff   12 Western - 12 with cross-cultural experience
4 non-Western - 4 with cross-cultural experience

Languages of instruction   English, Korean, Spanish

Learning styles   95% formal class-room teaching
5% non-formal learning experiences

Courses offered   Missiology degree at doctoral level
Missiology degree at master's level

Training ethos   We offer missological concentrations in :

Church growth, Anthropology, Leadership, History of mission, Translation, Judaic studies & Jewish evangelism, Urban ministry, Spirituality in global mission, general Missiology, International development, Islamics.

Every concentration is based on core competencies of Word, World & the Church.

Profile no. 238   United States Of America

Established 1891
GEORGE FOX COLLEGE

Mailing address   GEORGE FOX COLLEGE
Department of Religious Studies
414 N. Meridian # 6024
Newberg, OR   97132 - 2697 USA

Phone (503) 538 - 8383   **Fax** (503) 537 - 3834

Location   as above

Director of program   Dr Ronald G Stansell, Chair

Teaching staff   Western - with cross-cultural experience
non-Western - with cross-cultural experience

Languages of instruction   English

Learning styles   90% formal class-room teaching
10% non-formal learning experiences

Courses offered   World Mission courses in bachelor's degree

Training ethos   The formal, classroom teaching component includes development of critical thinking and writing skills and much discussion.

We offer majors in both International Studies and Christian Ministries which have "missions tracks" to them.

Profile no. 239 United States Of America

Established 1884-9
GORDON-CONWELL THEOLOGICAL SEMINARY

Mailing address GORDON-CONWELL THEOLOGICAL SEMINARY,
Department of Missions
130 Essex Street
South Hamilton, MA   01982 USA

Phone (508) 468 - 7111   **Fax** (508) 468 - 6691

Location as above

Director of program Gary J. Bekker, Assoc. Professor

Teaching staff 31 Western - 16 with cross-cultural experience
0 non-Western

Languages of instruction English

Learning styles 97% formal class-room teaching
3% non-formal learning experiences

Courses offered Missiology degree at master's level
Pre-field training & orientation - 20 weeks

Training ethos Gordon-Conwell Theological Seminary prepares men and women for ministry in their home context and for intercultural ministry.

We stress a strong academic foundation combined with a rich supervised field-based ministry experience.

Profile no. 240   United States Of America

Established 1943
GRACE COLLEGE OF THE BIBLE

Mailing address GRACE COLLEGE OF THE BIBLE
Intercultural Ministry Major
Ninth & William
Omaha, NE   68108 USA

Phone (402) 449 - 2800   **Fax** (402) 341 - 9587

Location as above

Director of program Jared Burkholder, Chair

Teaching staff 2 Western - 2 with cross-cultural experience
0 non-Western

Languages of instruction English

Learning styles 88% formal class-room teaching
12% non-formal learning experiences

Courses offered World Mission courses in bachelor's degree
World Mission courses at certificate or diploma level

Training ethos It is very possible that by 1996 we will be offering 19 hours of the 24 hours intercultural component (79%) on-site in the Republic of Mali in cooperation with the Gospel Missionary Union.

This innovation would be offered every other year, from June through mid December. It could be taken as an independent component or as part of a degree program.

Profile no. 241 United States Of America

Established 1941
GRAND RAPIDS BAPTIST SEMINARY

Mailing address GRAND RAPIDS BAPTIST SEMINARY
100 East Beltline, NE
Grand Rapids, MI 49505 USA

Phone (616) 949 5300   **Fax** (616) 949 4154

Location as above

Director of program Dr Paul A Beals, Prof. of Missiology

Teaching staff 2 Western - 2 with cross-cultural experience
0 non-Western

Languages of instruction English

Learning styles 70% formal class-room teaching
30% non-formal learning experiences

Courses offered Missiology track in D.Min
Missiology degree at master's level
World Mission courses in bachelor's degree

Training ethos * To integrate missiological instruction with the Biblical, theological, historical and language study offered by our seminary to enable the student to "do theology" in today's global cultural milieu.

* To contextualize missiological instruction to enable the student to evangelize, edify believers and establish churches in both urban and pioneer settings.

* To encourage the development of national leaders in formal, non-formal and informal settings.

Profile no. 242					United States Of America

Established 1952
HARDING UNIVERSITY GRADUATE SCHOOL OF RELIGION

Mailing address HARDING UNIVERSITY GRADUATE SCHOOL OF
RELIGION
1000 Cherry Road
Memphis, TN   38117 USA

Phone (901) 761 1350   **Fax** (901) 761 1356

Location as above

Director of program Dr Evertt W Huffard, Prof. of Missiology

Teaching staff 1 Western - 1 with cross-cultural experience
0 non-Western

Languages of instruction English

Learning styles 90% formal class-room teaching
10% non-formal learning experiences

Courses offered Missiology degree at master's level

Training ethos Graduate training in missiology at HUGSR seeks to equip M.Div. graduates to develop sending churches and to be involved themselves in cross-cultural ministry.

A student can specialize in missiological studies in the MA program.

Profile no. 243 **United States Of America**

Established 1967
IICC - INSTITUTE FOR INTERNATIONAL CHRISTIAN COMMUNICATION

Mailing address IICC - INSTITUTE FOR INTERNATIONAL CHRISTIAN COMMUNICATION
PO Box 14519
Portland, OR   97215 USA

Phone (503) 234 1639   **Fax** (503) 234 1639

Location as above

Director of program Dr Donald K. Smith, Director

Teaching staff 6 Western - 6 with cross-cultural experience
3 non-Western - 3 with cross-cultural experience

Languages of instruction English

Learning styles 35% formal class-room teaching
65% non-formal learning experiences

Courses offered World Mission courses at diploma or certificate level
Pre-field training & orientation - 2 to 6 weeks
In-service training : 1 to 4 weeks in the field

Training ethos IICC conducts in-service workshops for missionaries from and to every nation and culture, dealing especially with problems of missionary stress, cross-cultural communication and problems (and opportunities !) from the interaction of culture and ministry.

Workshops are planned on the invitation of mission groups.

Profile no. 244 United States Of America

Established 1987
INTERNATIONAL CENTER FOR URBAN TRAINING

Mailing address INTERNATIONAL CENTER for URBAN TRAINING
PO Box 143
San Jose, CA   95103 USA

Phone (408) 998 4770   **Fax** (408) 292 9406

Location   2302 Zanker, San Jose

Director of program   Dr Roy Thompson

Teaching staff   6 Western - 6 with cross-cultural experience
2 non-Western - 2 with cross-cultural experience

Languages of instruction   English

Learning styles   20% formal class-room teaching
80% non-formal learning experiences

Courses offered   Missiology degree at master's level
World Mission courses in bachelor's degree
World Mission courses at certificate or diploma level
Pre-field training & orientation - 8 weeks or 9 months

Training ethos   Focus is on urban cross-cultural ministry.

Supervised internship under an ethnic leader.

Over 30 ethnic non-western people groups to minister in.

Training can be individual or agency specific.

Profile no. 245 United States Of America

Established 1960
INTERNATIONAL TEAMS

Mailing address INTERNATIONAL TEAMS
PO Box 203
Prospect Heights, IL   60070 USA

Phone (708) 870 3800   **Fax** (708) 870 3399

Location   515 Schoenbeck Road, Prospect Heights

Director of program   Richard R. Becker, Director of Training

Teaching staff   5 Western - 5 with cross-cultural experience
0 non-Western

Languages of instruction   We use outside resources for 10 languages

Learning styles   75% formal class-room teaching
25% non-formal learning experiences

Courses offered   Pre-field training & orientation - 4 months

Training ethos   International Teams exists to make Jesus Christ known and
to see lives transformed by the power of God.

We emphasize evangelism, showing compassion and developing people.

To achieve this we organize teams, provide training and personalized care to team members and encourage innovation in ministry.

Profile no. 246   United States Of America

Established 1893
JOHNSON BIBLE COLLEGE
CROSS-CULTURAL MINISTRIES

Mailing address JOHNSON BIBLE COLLEGE
Cross-cultural Ministries
7900 Johnson Drive
Knoxville TN 37998 USA

Phone (615) 577 4017   **Fax** (615) 579 2337

Location as above

Director of program Norman M. Dungan

Teaching staff 4 Western - 3 with cross-cultural experience
0 non-Western

Languages of instruction English

Learning styles 75% formal class-room teaching
25% non-formal learning experiences

Courses offered World Mission courses in bachelor's degree

Training ethos The cross-cultural program is composed of two specialities

One is a traditional Missions program, with a Bible major and a thorough missions curriculum of 18 hours plus an additional 3-6 hours of specialty-related electives.
A 3 hour cross-cultural internship is required.

The other is a program in Teaching English to Speakers of Other Languages. (TESOL)
This is offered in 4 formats : as an add-on to the college's Elementary Education major; as a specialty (18 hours); as an add-on to the Missions specialty; and as a certificate program for Christian workers with significant cross-cultural experience.
In this final format 5 hours may be taken by correspondence and 5 hours in a 3 week summer session. Field experience is incorporated into the final 5 hour component.

Profile no. 247 United States Of America

Established 1933
LANCASTER BIBLE COLLEGE

Mailing address LANCASTER BIBLE COLLEGE
9001 Eden Road
Lancaster, PA 17601 USA

Phone (717) 569 7071 **Fax** (717) 560 8216

Location as above

Director of program Sanford Good, Chair

Teaching staff 2 Western - 2 with cross-cultural experience

Languages of instruction English

Learning styles 60% formal class-room teaching
40% non-formal learning experiences

Courses offered World Mission courses in bachelor's degree
World Mission courses at certificate or diploma level

Training ethos Everyone gets 48 hours of Bible; Christian Service in local ministries; 6 cross-cultural ministry teams are sent out each year; possibility of 15 hours credit for a semester in cross-cultural setting.

Required cross-cultural internship for missions students.

3 credit course on prayer as foundation missions course.

High non-formal emphasis

Profile no. 248 United States Of America

Established 1923
LIFE BIBLE COLLEGE

Mailing address LIFE BIBLE COLLEGE
World Mission Department
1100 W. Covina Blvd.
San Dimas CA 91773 USA

Phone (909) 599 5433   **Fax** (714) 599 6690

Location suburban community of Los Angeles

Director of program Dr John Louwerse

Teaching staff 2.5 Western - all with cross-cultural experience
0 non-Western

Languages of instruction English

Learning styles 75% formal class-room teaching
25% non-formal learning experiences

Courses offered World Mission courses in bachelor's degree
World Mission courses at certificate or diploma level
Pre-field training & orientation - semester

Training ethos The cross-cultural ministry program serves as preparation for the student who anticipates any kind of ministry in a cross-cultural context, either within or outside the United States.

Profile no. 249 United States Of America

Established 1944
LINCOLN CHRISTIAN COLLEGE & SEMINARY

Mailing address LINCOLN CHRISTIAN COLLEGE & SEMINARY
World Missions Department
Box 178
Lincoln IL 62656 USA

Phone (217) 732 3168   **Fax** (217) 732 5914

Location 100 Campus View Drive, Lincoln

Director of program Mark Shelley, Chair

Teaching staff 4 Western - 4 with cross-cultural experience
0 non-Western

Languages of instruction English

Learning styles 90% formal class-room teaching
10% non-formal learning experiences

Courses offered Missiology degree at doctoral level
World Mission courses in bachelor's degree

Training ethos "Circling the Globe with the Gospel" is our guiding and motivation slogan.

Missiological-oriented courses include cultural analyses, interview projects and field experiences.

Cross-cultural internships from 10 weeks to 1 year are required.

Many additional ezperienes, including a "Week of Evangelism" each year are provided.

Profile no. 250 United States Of America

Established 1965
LINK CARE CENTER

Mailing address LINK CARE CENTER
1734 W. Shaw Avenue
Fresno, CA   93711 USA

Phone (209) 439 5920   **Fax** (209) 439 2214

Location as above

Director of program Dr Brent Lindquist, President

Teaching staff 6 Western - 4 with cross-cultural experience
0 non-Western

Languages of instruction English

Learning styles 25% formal class-room teaching
75% non-formal learning experiences

Courses offered Pre-field training & orientation - 3 weeks

Training ethos LEARNING TO LEAVE/LEAVING TO LEARN is a three week program designed to enable the new missionary to understand who they are, how they got that way and what they will need to continue their preparation for cross-cultural communicative competence.

Profile no. 251 United States Of America

Established 1944
LUTHERAN BIBLE INSTITUTE

Mailing address   LUTHERAN BIBLE INSTITUTE
4221 228th S.E.
Issaquah WA   98027 USA

Phone (206) 392 0400   **Fax**

Location   as above

Director of program   Patricia M Lelvis, Director

Teaching staff   All Western - half with cross-cultural experience
0 non-Western

Languages of instruction   English

Learning styles   65% formal class-room teaching
35% non-formal learning experiences

Courses offered   World Mission courses in bachelor's degree
World Mission courses at diploma or certificate level
Pre-field training & orientation - 2 weeks & 10 weeks

Training ethos   The Lutheran Bible Institute is an "institute"- which means it thinks of itself as a training center where the teachers are expected to be hands-on practitioners and the students are apprentices.

Profile no. 252   **United States Of America**

Established 1927
MANHATTAN CHRISTIAN COLLEGE

Mailing address   MANHATTAN CHRISTIAN COLLEGE
Cross-cultural Ministries
1415 Anderson Avenue
Manhattan, KS   66502 USA

Phone (913) 539 3571   **Fax**

Location   across the street from Kansas State University

Director of program   Prof. Rusty Thornley

Teaching staff   1 Western - 1 with cross-cultural experience
0 non-Western staff

Languages of instruction   English

Learning styles   80% formal class-room teaching
20% non-formal learning experiences

Courses offered   World Mission courses in bachelor's degree
World Mission courses at certificate or diploma level

Training ethos   We have cooperative and dual-degree programs with Kansas State University in such areas as cross-cultural ministry with pre-nursing; and cross-cultural ministry with Public Health and Nutrition.

Profile no. 253				United States Of America

Established
MID-AMERICA BAPTIST THEOLOGICAL SEMINARY

Mailing address MID-AMERICA BAPTIST THEOLOGICAL SEMINARY
PO Box 3624
Memphis, TN 38173-0624 USA

                   Phone   **Fax**

Location

Director of program Dr. Donald R. Dunavant

Teaching staff 4 Western - 3 with cross-cultural experience
0 non-Western

Languages of instruction English

Learning styles

Courses offered D,Theol. with a major inMissions
D.Min. in Missiology
M.Div. with an emphasis on Missions

Training ethos To integrate the classical disciplines of Biblical, historical, theological, social and linguistic studies with those significant tasks of the missionary practitioner.

To provide theoretical and practical assistance to the missionary who has a broad range of field responsibilities, who faces complex cross-cultural challenges and who is committed to involvement in evangelism that results in churches.

Profile no. 254   United States Of America

Established 1954
MISSIONARY INTERNSHIP

Mailing address   MISSIONARY INTERNSHIP
P O Box 50110
Colorado Springs, CO   80949   USA

Phone (719) 594 0687   **Fax** (719) 594 4682

Location   5245 Centennial Blvd., Suite 202

Director of program   Paul E. Nelson, President

Teaching staff   9 Western - 9 with cross-cultural experience
1 non-Western with cross-cultural experience

Languages of instruction   English

Learning styles   70% formal class-room teaching
30% non-formal learning experiences

Courses offered   Pre-field training & orientation - from 2 to 9 weeks

Training ethos   Missionary Internship programs provide cross-cultural training focusing on growth in the personal, interpersonal, intercultural and spiritual dimensions.

The approach used is that of personalizing the information, aiming at heart issues, integrating the entire experience and individual reflection on what is being learned.

Profile no. 255   United States Of America

Established 1886
MOODY BIBLE INSTITUTE,

Mailing address MOODY BIBLE INSTITUTE
Department of World Missions & Evangelism
820 N. La Salle Blvd.
Chicago, IL   60610-3284 USA

Phone (312) 329 4420   **Fax** (312) 329 4359

Location in the centre of Chicago

Director of program Ray Badgero, Chairman

Teaching staff 9 Western - 9 with cross-cultural experience
0 non-Western

Languages of instruction English - some Spanish

Learning styles 60% formal class-room teaching
40% non-formal learning experiences

Courses offered Missiology degree at master's level
World Mission courses in bachelor's degree

Training ethos A Mentoring, Field-based instructional model using rhe cultural groups of Chicago and faculty-directed non-western countries.

A balance of theory and practice with a solid foundation in Bible.

Profile no. 256 United States Of America

Established 1936
MULTNOMAH BIBLE COLLEGE

Mailing address MULTNOMAH BIBLE COLLEGE
8435 NE Glisan Street
Portland, OR   97220 USA

Phone (503) 255 - 0332   **Fax** (503) 254 - 1268

Location as above

Director of program Dr. Thomas J. Kopp, Missions Advisor

Teaching staff 45 Western - 23 with cross-cultural experience
0 non-Western

Languages of instruction English

Learning styles 90% formal class-room teaching
10% non-formal learning experiences

Courses offered World Mission courses in bachelor's degree

Training ethos Bible is the heart of Multnomah's curriculum and the heart of the Bible is missions.

Believing that those who study the bible honestly and seriously will become missions-minded, it is the objective of the intercultural studies concentration to equip students for effective cross-cultural living and ministry.

This is accomplished by integrating historical, theological, anthropological and missiological studies with practical ministry assignments and internships.

Profile no. 257　　　　　　　　　　United States Of America

Established 1992
MUSLIM WORLD INTERNSHIP

Mailing address　MUSLIM WORLD INTERNSHIP
INTERCULTURAL EFFECTIVENESS
17272 Dorset
Southfield, MI 48075 USA

Phone (810) 557 1953　　**Fax**

Location　as above

Director of program　David L Fogleboch, Director

Teaching staff　1 Western
1 non-Western

Languages of instruction　English

Learning styles　30% formal class-room teaching
70% non-formal learning experiences

Courses offered

Training ethos　The Muslim World Internship is designed to complement your schooling with practical real life ministry in the Middle Eastern Muslim community (100,000 population) in metro-Detroit.

Direct work with a mentor involved in Muslim ministry.

Profile no. 258   United States Of America

Established 1987
NAZARENE THEOLOGICAL SEMINARY
SCHOOL OF WORLD MISSION & EVANGELISM

Mailing address NAZARENE THEOLOGICAL SEMINARY
School of World Mission & Evangelism
1700 E. Mever Blvd.
Kansas City, MO   64131 USA

Phone (816) 333 6254   **Fax** (816) 333 6271

Location as above

Director of program Dr. Charles Gailey, Director

Teaching staff 6 Western - 5 with cross-cultural experience
0 non-Western

Languages of instruction English

Learning styles 85% formal class-room teaching
15% non-formal learning experiences

Courses offered Missiology degree at master's level
Pre-field training & orientation - 3 months

Training ethos Seventy students from various denominations are being educated for missionary service in this school.

Every student participates in an "on-site" nternship program in a Korean, Spanish, Cambodian, African, American or other ethnic congregation, thus crossing cultural boundaries while in training.

Profile no. 259 United States Of America

Established 1944
NEBRASKA CHRISTIAN COLLEGE

Mailing address   NEBRASKA CHRISTIAN COLLEGE
1800 Syracuse Avenue
Norfolk, NE   68701 USA

Phone (402) 371 5960   **Fax** (402) 371 5967

Location   as above

Director of program   Ray Stites, President

Teaching staff   8 Western - 1 with cross-cultural experience
0 non-Western

Languages of instruction   English

Learning styles

Courses offered   World Mission courses in bachelor's degree

Training ethos   Nebraska Christian College offers degree programs with a major in Bible and an emphasis in cross-cultural missions.

Profile no. 260　　　　　　　　　　　　　　United States Of America

Established 1950
NORTH AMERICAN BAPTIST SEMINARY

Mailing address　NORTH AMERICAN BAPTIST SEMINARY
　　　　　　　　　　1321 West 22nd Street
　　　　　　　　　　Sioux Falls, SD　　57105 USA

　　　　　　Phone (605) 336 6588　　**Fax** (605) 335 9090

Location　　　as above

Director of program　Dr George W Lang, Assoc. Professor

Teaching staff　13 Western - 7 with cross-cultural experience
　　　　　　　　　0 non-Western

Languages of instruction　English

Learning styles　90% formal class-room teaching
　　　　　　　　　10% non-formal learning experiences

Courses offered　MDiv with Missions Concentration.

Training ethos

Profile no. 261   United States Of America

Established 1891
NORTH PARK THEOLOGICAL SEMINARY

Mailing address   NORTH PARK THEOLOGICAL SEMINARY
3225 W. Foster Avenue
Chicago, IL   60625- 489 5 USA

Phone (312) 478 2696   **Fax** (312) 583 0858

Location   as above

Director of program   Dr Wayne C Weld, Professor of Missions

Teaching staff   2 Western - 2 with cross-cultural experience
0 non-Western

Languages of instruction   English

Learning styles   90% formal class-room teaching
10% non-formal learning experiences

Courses offered   Missiology degree at doctoral level

Training ethos   Traditional M. Div. program supplemented by local field trips and service/study project overseas.

Profile no. 262   United States Of America

Established 1903
NORTHWESTERN COLLEGE

Mailing address   NORTHWESTERN COLLEGE
3003 Snelling Avenue N.
Roseville, MN 55113 USA

Phone (612) 631 5193   **Fax** (612) 631 5124

Location   as above

Director of program   Dr. Donald Ericksen, President

Teaching staff   4 Western - 4 with cross-cultural experience
1 non-Western - 1 with cross-cultural experience

Languages of instruction   English

Learning styles   95% formal class-room teaching
5% non-formal learning experiences

Courses offered   World Mission courses in bachelor's degree

Training ethos   A Liberal Arts/Bible/Vocation approach to cross-cultural ministries with a particular emphasis on social sciences, applied thought, the missionary task.

Profile no. 263   United States Of America

Established
OAK HILLS BIBLE COLLEGE

Mailing address   OAK HILLS BIBLE COLLEGE
Intercultural Studies
1600 Oak Hills Rd. S.W.
Bemidji, MN   56601-3034 USA

Phone (218) 751 8670   **Fax** (218) 751 8825

Location   as above

Director of program   Greg Giles, Director

Teaching staff   23 Western - 8 with cross-cultural experience
0 non-Western

Languages of instruction   English

Learning styles   90% formal class-room teaching
10% non-formal learning experiences

Courses offered   World Mission courses in bachelor's degree
World Mission courses at diploma or certificate level

Training ethos   OHBC employs a rural venue and traditional classroom instruction in a small community to prepare Christians to live, work & serve as laymen, Pastors & missionaries in a multi-cultural world.

Low student-teacher ratios allow modelling and attention to integration of acquired knowledge and skills.

Profile no. 264　　　　　　　　　　　　　　United States Of America

Established 1910
OKHLAHOMA BAPTIST UNIVERSITY

Mailing address　OKHLAHOMA BAPTIST UNIVERSITY
　　　　　　　　　　500 W. University
　　　　　　　　　　Shawnee, OK　　74801 USA

　　　　　　　　　　Phone (405) 878 2229　　**Fax** (405) 878 2069

Location　　　　　40 miles east of Oklahoma City

Director of program　Dr Dick Rader, Dean

Teaching staff　　10 Western - 6 with cross-cultural experience
　　　　　　　　　　0 non-Western

Languages of instruction　English

Learning styles　98% formal class-room teaching
　　　　　　　　　　2% non-formal learning experiences

Courses offered　World Mission courses in bachelor's degree

Training ethos　We offer a traditional liberal arts education with a major
　　　　　　　　　　of 30 hours in missions and related minors of 18 hour in
　　　　　　　　　　Asian Studies and Anthropology, all within a
　　　　　　　　　　distinctively Christian environment.

Profile no. 265 United States Of America

Established 1965
ORAL ROBERTS UNIVERSITY

Mailing address ORAL ROBERTS UNIVERSITY
School of Theology & Missions
7777 S. Lewis Avenue
Tulsa, OK   74171 USA

Phone (918) 495 6096   **Fax** (918) 495 6033

Location as above

Director of program Dr Paul G Chappell, Dean

Teaching staff 4 Western - 4 with cross-cultural experience
0 non-Western

Languages of instruction English

Learning styles 80% formal class-room teaching
20% non-formal learning experiences

Courses offered Missiology degree at master's level
World Mission courses in bachelor's degree

Training ethos The Master of Arts In Missions is a specialized program designed to train competent professionals to carry the saving/healing Gospel to the uttermost bounds of the earth.

The program is offered in an evangelical charismatic environment and presents a well-rounded philosophy of missions with emphasis on Biblical principles, the ministry of healing, evangelism, church planting and methods of effective cross-cultural comunication.

Pratical mission experience is part of the program.

This program is accredited by the Association of Theological schools in the United States and Canada.

Profile no. 266   United States Of America

Established
PACIFIC CHRISTIAN COLLEGE

Mailing address   PACIFIC CHRISTIAN COLLEGE
Intercultural Studies Degree
2500 E Nutwood
Fullerton, CA   92631 USA

Phone (714) 879 3901   **Fax** (714) 526 0231

Location   as above

Director of program   Prof. Sherman S Pemberton, Chair

Teaching staff   3 Western - 3 with cross-cultural experience
1 non-Western - 1 with cross-cultural experience

Languages of instruction   English & Spanish

Learning styles   80% formal class-room teaching
20% non-formal learning experiences

Courses offered   Missiology degree at master's level
World Mission courses in bachelor's degree
World Mission courses at certificate or diploma level
Pre-field training & orientation - 1 week each

Training ethos   Centered on the Biblical model with priority given to perceptions of target peoples.

3 on field cities approved for 1 year practicum with option of a second year leading to MA credit.

Profile no. 267   United States Of America

Established 1985
REGENT UNIVERSITY, SCHOOL OF DIVINITY

Mailing address   REGENT UNIVERSITY
School of Divinity
1000 Centerville Turnpike
Virginia Beach, VA 23464 - 5041 USA

Phone (804) 523 7984   **Fax** (804) 424 7051

Location   as above

Director of program   Dr. Howard L Foltz, Prof. GlobalEvangelism

Teaching staff   3 Western - 3 with cross-cultural experience
0 non-Western

Languages of instruction   English

Learning styles   90% formal class-room teaching
10% non-formal learning experiences

Courses offered   Missiology degree at master's level

Training ethos   In the Regent School of Divinity, academic and spiritual pursuits are considered inseparable components of a good education. So classes are conducted in an atmosphere where academic issues are confronted through an informed and vibrant faith.

The School of Divinity maintains a strong Biblical, theological foundation to support pre-eminent programs of leadership training in church revitalization and in global evangelization.

This emphasis reflects the faculty's belief that a Biblical and theological education is not an end in itself, but should be expressed in the life of the Church and its outreach to the world.

Profile no. 268   United States Of America

Established 1946
RIO GRANDE BIBLE INSTITUTE

Mailing address   RIO GRANDE BIBLE INSTITUTE
4300 S. Business 281

Edinburgh, TX   78539 USA

Phone (210) 380 8100   **Fax** (210) 380 8256

Location   as above

Director of program   Bob Kasper

Teaching staff   18 Western - 12 with cross-cultural experience
5 non-Western - 2 with cross-cultural experience

Languages of instruction   Spanish

Learning styles   100% formal class-room teaching

Courses offered   World Mission courses in bachelor's degree

Training ethos   Mission emphasis is a minor of our B A in Biblical studies.
It involves 8 semester hours in theoretical courses, coupled with Christian service practicums.

Profile no. 269   United States Of America

Established 1948
ROANOKE BIBLE COLLEGE

Mailing address   ROANOKE BIBLE COLLEGE
Cross-cu;ltural Studies Department
714 1st Street
Elizabeth City, NC   27909 USA

Phone (919) 338 5191   **Fax** (919) 338 0801

Location   as above

Director of program   Professor Linda Joyner

Teaching staff   1 Western with cross-cultural experience
0 non-Western

Languages of instruction   English

Learning styles   85% formal class-room teaching
15% non-formal learning experiences

Courses offered   World Mission courses in bachelor's degree
World Mission courses at certificate or diploma level
Pre-field training & orientation -

Training ethos

Profile no. 270   **United States Of America**

Established 1994
SOUTHEASTERN BIBLE COLLEGE

Mailing address   SOUTHEASTERN BIBLE COLLEGE
Department of World Missions
3001 Highway 280 E.
Birmingham, AL 35243 USA

Phone (205) 969 0880   **Fax** (205) 970 9207

Location   as above

Director of program   Dr Hugh Huguley, Chairman Dept.

Teaching staff   2 Western - 2 with cross-cultural experience
0 non-Western

Languages of instruction   English

Learning styles   90% formal class-room teaching
10% non-formal learning experiences

Courses offered   World Mission courses in bachelor's degree

Training ethos   "It is the purpose of the Missions Program to give thorough preparation for prospective missionary condidates".

Profile no. 271 United States Of America

Established 1907
TOCCOA FALLS COLLEGE
SCHOOL OF WORLD MISSIONS

Mailing address TOCCOA FALLS COLLEGE
School of World Missions
PO Box 800297
Toccoa Falls, GA 30598 USA

Phone (706) 886 6831   **Fax** (706) 886 0210

Location as above

Director of program Norman E. Allison

Teaching staff 5 Western - 5 with cross-cultural experience
0 non-Western

Languages of instruction English

Learning styles 95% formal class-room teaching
5% non-formal learning experiences

Courses offered World Mission courses in bachelor's degree

Training ethos The School of World Missions is specifically designed to train missionaries in two different majors:

Missiology, for full-time church-related ctoss-cultural ministry ; and

Cross-Cultural Studies, designed for non-professional "Tentmakers" with a special emphasis in TESOL (Teaching English as a Second Lanaguage).

Strong emphasis in Bible, Anthropology and Missions.

At present about 100 people are majoring in the School of World Missions.

Profile no. 272 United States Of America

Established
TRINITY EVANGELICAL DIVINITY SCHOOL
SCHOOL OF WORLD MISSION AND EVANGELISM

Mailing address TRINITY EVANGELICAL DIVINITY SCHOOL
School of World Mission and Evangelism
2065 Half Dav Road &
Deerfield, IL   60015 USA

Phone (708) 317 8125   **Fax** (708) 317 8141

Location as above

Director of program Dr. Paul Hiebert, Chairman

Teaching staff 8 Western - 8 with cross-cultural experience
2 non-Western - 2 with cross-cultural experience

Languages of instruction English

Learning styles 70% formal class-room teaching
30% non-formal learning experiences

Courses offered Missiology degree at doctoral level
Missiology degree at master's level

Training ethos The SWME at Trinity Evangelical Divinity School is an evangelical school committed to building missions vision and competence through community life and learning.

Students and faculty work together in classes, small groups and joint chapels to help one another examine the mission of the church in the world in the light of the Gospel.

Interaction between mid-career missionaries, missions candidates and faculty with mission experience fosters discussions that lead to the integration of theory and practice, research and findings, and Biblical norms and cultural settings.

The school is committed to the authority of Scripture and to a sensitivity to human cultures.

Profile no. 273 United States Of America

Established 1935
WESTERN BAPTIST COLLEGE

Mailing address   WESTERN BAPTIST COLLEGE
5000 Deer Park Drive SE
Salem, OR   97301-9392 USA

Phone (503) 581 8600   **Fax** (503) 585 4316

Location   as above

Director of program   Prof. Robert W Wright

Teaching staff   60 Western - 10 with cross-cultural experience
0 non-Western

Languages of instruction   English

Learning styles   95% formal class-room teaching
5% non-formal learning experiences

Courses offered   World Mission courses in bachelor's degree
Pre-field training & orientation - 3 months

Training ethos   Majors & Minors in Missiology, overseas teaching (credential earned) in elementary & secondary education, cross-cultural counselling.

Profile no. 274   United States Of America

Established 1927
WESTERN SEMINARY
DIVISION OF INTERCULTURAL STUDIES

Mailing address WESTERN SEMINARY
Division of Intercultural Studies
5511 SE Hawthrones Blvd.
Portland, OR   97215 USA

Phone (503) 233 8561   **Fax** (503) 239 4216

Location as above

Director of program Dr Donald K Smith, Chair

Teaching staff 6 Western - all with cross-cultural experience
3 non-Western - all with cross-cultural experience

Languages of instruction English

Learning styles 95% formal class-room teaching
 5% non-formal learning experiences

Courses offered Missiology degree at doctoral level
Missiology degree at master's level
World Mission courses at certificate or diploma level
Pre-field training & orientation - 2 to 6 weeks

Training ethos Western's Division of Intercultural Studies is staffed by 5 full-time faculty, with an average of 23 years each of overseas service.

The Word of God is the foundation of the study, recognizing our task is to create understanding across cultural boundaries of the Gospel of Christ. Thus communication is at the core of the mission curriculum.

Intercultural studies are built on sound Biblical, theological knowledge and spiritual maturity.

Profile no. 275   United States Of America

Established 1929
WESTMINSTER THEOLOGICAL SEMINARY URBAN MISSIONS PROGRAM

Mailing address   WESTMINSTER THEOLOGICAL SEMINARY
Urban Missions Program
P O Box 27009
Philadelphia, PA   19118 USA

Phone (215) 889 5511   **Fax** (215) 887 5404

Location   as above

Director of program   Manuel Ortiz, Director

Teaching staff   2 Western - 2 with cross-cultural experience
0 non-Western

Languages of instruction   English

Learning styles   90% formal class-room teaching
10% non-formal learning experiences

Courses offered   Missiology degree at doctoral level
Missiology degree at master's level
World Mission courses in bachelor's degree

Training ethos   The focus of our studies is on missions to the global cities.

In a 3 year cycle of teaching, we offer a minimin of 27 courses focusing on ministry in US and global cities.

In addition to our full time staff, we use 7 part time lecturers.

We publish the quarterly journal Urban Mission (Harvie Conn, editor) and the quarterly Urban Mission Newsletter.

Profile no. 276 United States Of America

Established 1972
WHEATON COLLEGE
INSTITUTE FOR CROSS-CULTURAL TRAINING

Mailing address WHEATON COLLEGE
Institute for Cross-cultural Training
812 N President
Wheaton, IL 60187 USA

Phone (708) 762 5164   **Fax** (708) 752 5935

Location as above

Director of program Dr Doug McConnell, Chair of Dept.

Teaching staff 9 Western - 8 with cross-cultural experience
0 non-Western

Languages of instruction English

Learning styles 80% formal class-room teaching
20% non-formal learning experiences

Courses offered Missiology degree at master's level
Pre-field training & orientation - 4 weeks

Training ethos Emphasis is placed on the theological, Biblical, historical and practical aspects of missiology.

Every student learns how to do research and strategic planning.

Optional emphases include: leadership, world religions, evangelism, urban studies/mission, development.

Profile no. 277 United States Of America

Established 1986
WORLD INSTITUTE FOR CROSS- CULTURAL EVANGELISM STUDIES

Mailing address WORLD INSTITUTE for CROSS- CULTURAL EVANGELISM STUDIES
PO Box 4100
Cincinnati,OH   45204-4100 USA

Phone (513) 244 8149   **Fax** (513) 244 8430

Location   2700 Glenway Avenue, Cincinnati

Director of program   Doug Lucas, Co-ordinator

Teaching staff   7 Western - 7 with cross-cultural experience
0 non-Western

Languages of instruction   English

Learning styles   75% formal class-room teaching
25% non-formal learning experiences

Courses offered   Courses on World Mission in bachelor's degree
Courses on World Mission at certificate or diploma level
Pre-field training & orientation - 10 days

Training ethos   The World Institute for Cross-cultural Evangelism/Studies utilizes materials developed by:

a) Missionary Internship, including the Entry Posture Model

b) The Brewsters including the LAMP Method

c) Cell group Church-Planting Specialists including some of our own in-house researchers

d) Cross-cultural research and debriefing performed with our own 300+ students over the last 7 years

The learning follows a style where many lectures are presented, then appplied through the consideration of case studies, learning activities and simulations.

Profile no. 278　　　　　　　　　　　　　　　　　　　　　　Vanuatu

Established 1988
TALUA MINISTRY TRAINING CENTRE

Mailing address　TALUA MINISTRY TRAINING CENTRE
　　　　　　　　　PO Box 242
　　　　　　　　　Santo VANUATU

　　　　　　　　　Phone　　　　　　　　**Fax**

Location　　　as above

Director of program　Pastor Kalsakau Urtalo, Principal

Teaching staff　4 Western - 1 with cross-cultural experience
　　　　　　　　5 non-Western - none with cross-cultural experience

Languages of instruction　English & Bislama

Learning styles　60% formal class-room teaching
　　　　　　　　40% non-formal learning experiences

Courses offered　World Mission courses at certificate or diploma level
　　　　　　　　Pre-field training & orientation - 4 weeks annually

Training ethos　In the centre a programme for training the wives of the students was introduced to be trained in the Ministry together with their hausbands.

Profile no. 279   Venezuela,

Established 1988
OPERACION TIMOTEO

Mailing address OPERACION TIMOTEO
c/o Depto de Capacitation
Apartado 16377
Caracas 1011-A VENEZUELA

Phone 58-2 577 9019   **Fax** 58-2 762 6155

Location as above
extension centers in some other cities

Director of program Gloria Garcia Delgado, Instructor

Teaching staff 2 Western - 2 with cross-cultural experience
12 non-Western - 5 with cross-cultural experience

Languages of instruction Spanish

Learning styles 25% formal class-room teaching
75% non-formal learning experiences

Courses offered World Mission courses in bachelor's degree
World Mission courses at certificate or diploma level
Pre-field training & orientation

Training ethos Operacion Timoteo seeks to prepare Latin American missionaries for cross-cultural ministry combining spiritual formation, practical experience and missiological reflection in order to work among the less evangelized groups of people in the world.

Our programs are focussed in different areas, among them :

Perspectives on the World Christian Movement; Discipleship School; Evangelization of the Muslim World; Evangelization of Tribal groups; and Missionary internships to minorities in Venezuela & the Caribbean Islands.

Profile no. 280   **Venezuela,**

Established 1969
SEMINARIO EVANGELICO ASOCIADO

Mailing address SEMINARIO EVANGELICO ASOCIADO
Apartado 2050
Maracay, Aragua 2101 A, VENEZUELA

Phone 43 839 273   **Fax** 43 839 273

Location Avda. Principal #143, El Limon, Maracay

Director of program Lic. Custodio Lopez

Teaching staff 6 Western - 6 with cross-cultural experience
6 non-Western - 1 with cross-cultural experience

Languages of instruction Spanish

Learning styles 60% formal class-room teaching
40% non-formal learning experiences

Courses offered World Mission courses in bachelor's degree
World Mission courses at certificate or diploma level

Training ethos SEA has 3 programs:

1 Pastoral ministry
2 Urban cross cultural missions
3 Mission to indigenous peoples

We try to integrate academics with ministry experiences and spiritual growth.

Our courses are available at the resident seminary location as well at extension centers.

Profile no. 281   Zaire

Established
EVANGELICAL CHURCH NEW LIFE IN JESUS CHRIST

Mailing address   Ecole Superieure de Theologie Evangelique
B.P. 6289 Lubumbashi 10,
Region du Shaba ZAIRE

                       Phone   **Fax**

Location   Rue Kalongue No. 118, Katuba III, Lubumbashi

Director of program   Bishop Musenge Ngabu Kasongo

Teaching staff   12 Western - 5 with cross-cultural experience
3 non-Western - 1 with cross-cultural experience

Languages of instruction   French

Learning styles

Courses offered   Missiology degree at doctoral level - 5 years
World Mission courses in bachelor's degree - 3 years
World Mission courses at Diploma level - 2 years

Training ethos